Learn the Nautical Rules of the Road

Paul Boissier

Learn the Nautical Rules of the Road

An Expert Guide to the COLREGs

Paul Boissier

WILEY NAUTICAL

This edition first published 2010
© 2010 Paul Boissier

Registered office
John Wiley & Sons Ltd, The Atrium, Southern Gate, Chichester, West Sussex, PO19 8SQ, United Kingdom

For details of our global editorial offices, for customer services and for information about how to apply for permission to reuse the copyright material in this book please see our website at www.wiley.com.

The right of the author to be identified as the author of this work has been asserted in accordance with the Copyright, Designs and Patents Act 1988.

Wiley also publishes its books in a variety of electronic formats. Some content that appears in print may not be available in electronic books.

Designations used by companies to distinguish their products are often claimed as trademarks. All brand names and product names used in this book are trade names, service marks, trademarks or registered trademarks of their respective owners. The publisher is not associated with any product or vendor mentioned in this book. This publication is designed to provide accurate and authoritative information in regard to the subject matter covered. It is sold on the understanding that the publisher is not engaged in rendering professional services. If professional advice or other expert assistance is required, the services of a competent professional should be sought.

Library of Congress Cataloging-in-Publication Data
Boissier, Paul.

Learn the nautical rules of the road: an expert guide to the COLREGs / Paul Boissier.
p. cm.
Includes index.
ISBN 978-0-470-74912-8 (pbk.: alk. paper)

1. Rule of the road at sea. 2. Navigation--Safety measures. I. Title.
VK371.B649 2010
623.88'84--dc22
2009045971

A catalogue record for this book is available from the British Library.

Set in Humnst777EU by Laserwords Private Limited, Chennai, India
Printed in Italy by Printer Trento, Trento

CONTENTS

To Susie

With my thanks to:

Commander Nigel Hare and Mike Shrives for their invaluable assistance

Foreword

Every person who takes any boat to sea, from a small rowing boat to the mighty Queen Mary 2, needs to know the International Regulations for Preventing Collision at Sea, the Maritime Rules of the Road. They have developed over generations into a highly effective system for avoiding collisions on the water and are as fundamental to good seamanship and navigation as reading a chart correctly or tying a bowline knot.

When I joined the Merchant Navy we were required to know these regulations by heart. Our leave was threatened if we could not recite the sections we had to learn each voyage, until we knew them all. It was a hard task, which took many evenings at sea, but for our examinations an error could have you sent back to sea for six months. The benefit was that when one found oneself alone on the bridge in charge of a watch and was unsure of what action to take to avoid a collision, one could fall back on ones memory. In time, of course, the actions to take, or not to take, became instinctive.

Few people would be word perfect these days, but it is the awareness of what the rules state that is important. There is a logic behind them once you start to study them, and they are laid out in this book so that they can be more easily understood, whether you are learning them for the first time, or just revising to brush up on one's familiarity. Seamen have to be practical, they are dealing with raw nature and their trade cannot be fully learned by studying in books; it is a hands-on profession, improved by experience. This book is written in the sensible style you would expect from a seaman for seamen.

My desire has always been to encourage everyone to take up boating and enjoy their time on the water. I want everyone to have as much enjoyment as I have had over the years. To enjoy boating fully you must feel confidence in yourself, and I think you will find this book will help you to enjoy your time with that greater confidence to fit in with other seafarers on the rivers, estuaries, seas and oceans in safety.

Sir Robin Knox-Johnston

1 Introduction

In 2003, I wrote a book called 'Understanding the Rule of the Road', which focused on the needs of recreational yachtsmen. For this more comprehensive volume, I have made three specific changes:

- I have increased the scope of the book to encompass all seafarers.
- I have included the November 2003 changes to the Collision Regulations, and
- I have changed the format, which will hopefully make it all a bit easier to take in.

Learning the Rules has never been a particularly pleasant task, but it can't be avoided if you want to spend time on the water, either professionally or for recreation. It takes a fair amount of effort and experience to develop an enduring familiarity, but it is neither as complex nor as daunting as it might seem at first sight. The trick is to try to understand why the Rules are written as they are. If you can do this, they will start to make sense and your decisions will become safer and more intuitive.

The trouble is that there is really no place left on the high seas for incompetent or irresponsible people. You absolutely have to know these Rules from first to last if you are going to stay safe – irrespective of the shape, size or purpose of the craft that you are using. Whenever you take to the water, other seamen expect you to fit in with the rich tapestry of maritime activity taking place around you, involving vessels of varying size, manoeuvrability, nationality, purpose and competence. No quarter is given for lack of experience; there are no 'L plates' on a ship, and from the start you must be able to manoeuvre in a way that other mariners can understand and relate to. Whether you are keeping a bridge watch on a large merchant ship, or merely taking the air as a day sailor on the Solent, you must know enough to behave intelligently, and to avoid putting people's lives at risk.

Years ago, when I was commanding a little diesel-powered submarine running out of Gosport, I brought her into harbour on a beautiful, calm early-summer's day. It was spring tides. There was a fair old stream running east-west at the entrance to the channel by Outer Spit Buoy, and right in the middle of the channel, gently stemming the tidal stream in the light breeze, was a small sailing boat with a middle-aged couple sitting in the cockpit. I was to the south of them, and they both had their backs to me, chatting away with cups of tea in their hands.

They were not keeping any sort of a lookout. Rather unfairly, I decided to sneak up on them. Before long, the bows of the submarine were overhanging the yacht – and they still hadn't seen me. One of the submarine's officers walked down to the bows and, clearing his throat, very politely asked them if they would mind moving to one side so that we could get past. Without a shadow of embarrassment, they agreed, and so we entered harbour.

Polite as we all were, there is no escaping the fact that these people were just plain incompetent, and the sea is not a good place for incompetence, because within a very short space of time you will end up frightening yourself and a lot of other people too.

The Collision Regulations (COLREGs)

A friend who joined the Royal Navy with me once explained why he had turned his back on a lucrative career as a criminal barrister, and chosen a life at sea. 'Because,' he said, 'the sea is the last hiding place of the incurable romantic.'

He was right. The sea is the last great wilderness, wide open and untamed. A lot of people, amateurs and professionals alike, go to sea because it is lonely, wild and exciting. When you get out of sight of the land, you realise just how vast it is. The great majority of the oceans are outside territorial waters, and you might well think that you could get by without rules of any kind, simply because there is so much sea and so few ships. Besides, who on earth has the authority to enforce the rules?

In a nutshell, we need the rules because we are all creatures of habit. Commercial shipping tends to stick in unmarked marine motorways called the shipping lanes, precisely because they are the shortest distance between two points. Fishing vessels quite often work in groups, and yachtsmen are little better. In the past, if your dead reckoning was like mine, you spent half of a Channel crossing trying to decide whether that bit of land over there was France or Alderney. Even when navigating warships there were periods when I was less certain of my precise position that I might have wished. But now navigation is so precise, and the routes from A to B so well defined, that shipping is more concentrated than ever before.

Most shipping is crammed into a tiny proportion of the earth's oceans, and in a number of areas you can find merchant ships, fishing vessels, yachts and other vessels existing happily alongside each other, all pursuing their separate agendas. The Rules set out the context in which the remarkable diversity of maritime activity can safely use the same stretch of water. Over the last 150 years[1], seamen have gradually developed a code of rules which has become widely accepted and fits easily alongside 'the ordinary practice of seamen.'

The Collision Regulations that we currently use are the result of this process. In their present form, they date back to 1972, with the addition of various amendments designed to take account of developments in the way we use the sea. They are administered by the International Maritime Organisation[2]. The IMO was set up by the United Nations in 1948 to promote safety at sea, and is committed to regulating the international maritime community. There are now 168 member states of the IMO, and it is because so many nations have signed up to the Rules that they enjoy such wide-ranging authority.

---

[1]The earliest manifestation of the Rules was the Steam Navigation Act of 1846, which contained just two rules. The first required a steam vessel that was about to pass another vessel in a narrow channel to leave that vessel to port. The second required steam vessels crossing on different courses to turn to starboard to avoid a collision. If only life was that simple to-day.

[2]www.imo.org.

You do need to refresh your familiarity with the Rules occasionally, because they develop gently with time. If, like me, you have been going to sea since the time when Noah was taking carpentry lessons, you may still think that 'safe speed' means stopping in half of your visibility distance. And if you remember learning that in a close quarters situation the two vessels are either 'burdened' or 'privileged', it is time for you to have another look at the Rules – they have changed!

The 2003 amendments[3] introduce 'Wing-In-Ground (WIG) craft which, in its operational mode, flies in close proximity to the surface by utilising surface-effect action'.[4] They also make a number of small adjustments to the detail of individual rules.

Your fellow seafarers – a mixed bag

If you are to consistently take the right decisions, you must recognise what other vessels are doing, and understand how they are likely to react in a given set of circumstances. I have set out some observations in the following paragraphs, but much of this comes from experience and anyone embarking on a career as a professional seaman could do much worse than to spend time – ideally at sea – in a wide variety of vessels, to better understand the pressures and constraints of their fellow seafarers.

Merchant Ships

The great majority of vessels that you will encounter on the high seas will be merchant vessels. They will often have the most exotic provenance: owned in one country, flagged in another; officers and crew coming from a variety of places, and speaking a number of languages. But I have found most of them to be extremely professional in their conduct and operation. In deep water, they are slaves to an unforgiving schedule: I recently visited a container vessel which was about to leave Southampton and make a passage to Singapore. The Master showed me his itinerary which listed his arrival time at the Suez Canal, calculated to the nearest six minutes. These are not vessels with time to waste, and they will always tend to steer a straight course unless they have some good reason to alter. Despite that, however, in open waters they will generally take appropriate and timely action to avoid a close-quarters situation.

But you should recognise that the Officer of the Watch's field of view is often limited by the deck cargo, and in open waters the bridge normally has no more than two people on watch at any one time. The deck officer's job is to run the ship, operate the ship's radios, navigate . . . and be responsible for collision avoidance. If he is putting a fix on the chart, and his lookout just happens to be tying up his shoelaces, hunting for his sunglasses or dreaming about that delightful creature he met last month in Buenos Aires, the ship will not be in any position to take avoiding action.

---

[3]A list of recent amendments and their contents is attached at the end of Chapter 12.
[4]Rule 3(m).

Many vessels use electronic systems linked to the radar[5] or Automatic Identification System (AIS) to give warning of a developing close-quarters situation, which is fine as long as the system works, but it isn't entirely reliable.

A container ship in restricted waters.

But in any case, you should never assume that another vessel has seen you. You have no idea how competent they are, how good their lookout is, or whether the deck officer and the lookout even share a common language. You should treat everyone with suspicion until they prove you wrong: 99.9 per cent of the time, they will be fine, but the other 0.1 per cent could be expensive!

In inshore waters, nearly all big ships take a pilot with local knowledge to supplement the bridge team. Because of this, and because the waters are busier, the standard of lookout is likely to be pretty good. However, the effect is more than offset by the manoeuvring limitations of a big ship in shallow water. Just consider the draught. A large container ship can draw 50 feet (15 metres) or more, and that alone limits the pilot's freedom of manoeuvre. But that isn't his only constraint: tidal streams may be stronger and more variable close inshore, and the proximity of the bottom reduces the effectiveness of a ship's rudders and propellers. So, not only is navigation more complex, but his ability to turn or stop is also less than it would be in open waters. And this, of course, is where he is most likely to meet the greatest concentration of fishing vessels, ferries and enthusiastic, well-meaning but curious yachtsmen.

As if this weren't enough, the turning diameter of a big container ship may be as much as a third of a mile – more in shallow water – and any significant angle of rudder will induce a roll which increases the draught because of the rectangular section of the hull, sometimes by up to 2 metres. Since big ships often manoeuvre with minimal under-hull clearance when entering harbour, it could quite simply go aground if too much rudder is used.

Nor can it stop that easily. If the Captain of a large container vessel were to put the engine controls full astern at high speed, the flow of water over the propeller and torque limitations may even prevent the shaft from turning astern until the ship's speed had reduced significantly. Thereafter, it would take a mile or more to come to a halt. It is really little wonder than many merchant ships press on regardless: there is often little more that they can do.

Under these circumstances, big merchant ships do pretty well. But other, more manoeuvrable vessels should help them out where possible, particularly in restricted waters. If you can think

---

[5]ARPA – Automatic Radar Plotting Aid. Many small boat systems now also have this.

ahead and make a small, early alteration to avoid a close-quarters situation from developing you will have done your good deed for the day.

Fishing Boats

Fishing boats are a different problem altogether. They are hugely gregarious and often hang out in large groups. They are also massively constrained in their ability to manoeuvre when engaged in fishing. Even if you can't see their nets or lines, you can generally tell whether a boat is actually fishing or not by its speed. Most commercial fishing is conducted at 5 knots or less, which puts them on a par with a sailing boat. By contrast, when moving between fishing areas, or when they are coming home, they go like the clappers.

Just think about the skipper for a moment. He's out there, day and night, trying to earn an honest crust to feed his family. His boat will almost certainly be connected to impossibly complex structure consisting of wire, cordage, netting and heavy metal, which is valuable, unmanoeuvrable and potentially very dangerous. The tension on the trawl wires is measured in tons, and fishing boats often work in proximity to wrecks and other underwater obstructions. This is a demanding, tough job, conducted in all weathers on an unstable, slippery deck with a pervasive smell of fish entrails. It is only fair to treat them with a well-earned respect and keep clear of their bows and any wires or nets that they may be towing astern. If won't always be possible, but where you can find a way to sail round a fishing fleet, rather than through the middle, I would strongly advise you to do so.

If you are sailing in unfamiliar waters, it is often worth looking up the characteristics of the local fishing activity in the Admiralty Pilot, or another reliable reference book. I was once badly caught out in a submarine when making a dived passage through the Mediterranean. It was night time and I saw a succession of flashing white lights through the periscope, passing down each side of the submarine at a range of about half a mile. Over a 20-minute period, they progressively got closer, and it suddenly occurred to me that I was swimming gently into a large, static fishing net. Happily there was time to reverse course without snagging the nets and I escaped with little more than a bit of dented pride. The next morning when I looked in the Sailing Directions, I found that this kind of net was characteristic of the local tuna fishery, and a little advanced research would undoubtedly have saved me from a potentially awkward situation.

Warships

Warships are generally quite well-mannered; they keep a more-or-less reliable lookout and they are pretty good at adhering to the COLREGs. They are also, however, extremely unpredictable and will manoeuvre, turn, speed up and slow down to a rhythm of their own. They won't thank you for getting too close, even when they are at anchor, and they may occasionally tow things behind them without showing any shapes or lights. In particular, when refuelling at sea or when launching or recovering aircraft[6], they have only limited freedom of manoeuvre, and you should try to give them a wide berth.

---

[6]In this case, they would of course be Restricted in their Ability to Manoeuvre.

Warships can be quite intimidating for other seafarers, and their signals and flag hoists are not always designed to be understood by the average mariner. But on the whole they have complex agendas and tight deadlines to stick to, so they generally leave you in peace to get on with your business.

Yachtsmen

It is easy for professional seafarers to denigrate yachtsmen[7]. This may occasionally be deserved, but many are surprisingly competent and they are, after all, people who choose to spend a substantial part of their disposable income in order to go to sea – for the sheer enjoyment of doing so. Their vessels are by far the most manoeuvrable on the water, and they seldom have hard deadlines to make, so they ought to be able to keep out of trouble fairly easily. On the whole, though, they are very much less experienced than professional mariners, so both their fluency with the Rules, and their general awareness is often rusty.

So too is yachtsmen's capacity to assess other ships' movements. Their 'seaman's eye' is not as practised as that of a professional mariner; they have only limited capacity to accurately measure bearing movement, and with their radar and AIS are likely to give erratic predictions of (CPA)[8], even in a moderate sea. To further complicate matters, crew efficiency is often reduced in heavy weather, and they generally have no idea how difficult they are to see from a ship's bridge, especially at night. And I would never rely on a yacht to keep a perfect lookout, particularly astern.

It is also worth bearing in mind that sailing boats, when racing, conform (only within the racing fleet) to a wholly different set of rules – *the Racing Rules of Sailing* – and their movements may well be a little erratic as they manoeuvre for tactical advantage, or converge on a navigation mark. While none of this should prevent them from reacting to other shipping in accordance with the COLREGs, it is perhaps worth making some allowance for their preoccupation on the race, and giving them more space than the solitary cruising boat might require. In particular, when racing in light airs, they may be slow-moving and unwilling to start their engine for collision avoidance. They may therefore react rather later than other vessels in a similar position. You may be able to identify racing boats by the fact that, when racing, they seldom fly an ensign.

In short, yachtsmen are good and willing seafarers, but they cannot always be relied upon to take consistently predictable actions in a close-quarters situation and need to be treated with caution.

Human Factors in Collision Avoidance

Both the strongest and the weakest component of maritime safety is the individual: *you*. And individuals, even when experienced, may sometimes allow their performance or their concentration to fall off. Make a point of recognising this in yourself: the times when you are not firing on all cylinders, through tiredness, pressure, preoccupation, boredom, or even over-confidence. Prepare

---

[7]I have heard some big ship drivers – not the Royal Navy I hasten to add – rather unfairly referring to yachtsmen as WAFIs: wind-assisted complete idiots, and PAFIs: power-assisted complete idiots. If you are a yachtsman, do please try to exceed their expectations!

[8]CPA is the 'closest point of approach' – the minimum range between two vessels passing each other.

What you can do to make things easier

So, if these warnings have not put you off going to sea, I suppose nothing will. But there are things that you can do to make things easier and safer. Off the top of my head, a few practical suggestions would be:

1. **Keep a good lookout**. Look astern as well as ahead.
2. **Maintain a clear surface picture in your head.** Take into account traffic, your route, navigation hazards and the weather. Don't become fixated on one thing, no matter how close and ugly it is.
3. **Think ahead**. Work out how other ships are likely to behave, and take the necessary actions good and early.
4. **Be generous**. Often a small, early alteration can avoid a close-quarters situation arising at all. But when you have to alter course or speed in accordance with the Rules, do it boldly enough for the other vessel to notice, and make sure that you leave adequate separation.
5. **Trust your judgment.** Use electronic aids to support your eyes and your brain, not the other way round. By far the most reliable anti-collision device ever invented is the human eyeball properly supported by sound judgment, experience and intuition.
6. **Know the Rules thoroughly**. As well as learning the Rules, refresh your knowledge regularly.
7. **Always keep a watch on VHF Channel 16**. Keeping a good watch on VHF is an important part of 'keeping a good lookout' and can be almost as important as keeping a good visual lookout. There are times when talking to another ship (see Chapter 11) is useful for avoiding confusion, but don't rely on it. Keep the option to use VHF up your sleeve but always remember that the other guy may not be keeping a watch on VHF, or may not share your language, or indeed may not be in a position to implement any action that you propose. VHF communications are, of course, mandatory in some Vessel Traffic Service (VTS) areas. **But most importantly of all, you must always be prepared to question your assumptions and never – never be too proud to ask for help or advice, or to admit to a mistake.**

thoroughly so that you are familiar with the geography, your ship's handling characteristics, the weather, tides and currents, and the likely behaviour of other shipping. Know your limits, and be aware of when you are approaching the edge of your comfort zone.

Layout of this book

I have tried to make this book as user-friendly as I can. Most of the chapters are tied to specific rules, or blocks of rules, and where it is appropriate I have suggested that you read the particular rule or rules before starting on each chapter. Where it will help, I have included verbatim extracts of the Rules in the text, set into pale yellow text boxes.

I have also added my own comments and observations in pale blue boxes. Where I have done so, it must be recognised that these comments and observations are exactly that – my own – and they refer to the particular situation that I am describing. Manoeuvring for collision avoidance often involves more than the two vessels that are generally depicted in books like this – any manoeuvre that you make for one ship may well affect other vessels in your vicinity, and may also have implications on navigational safety. What you *actually* do in any particular set of circumstances is – and will always remain – a matter for your own personal judgment, balancing a number of wider considerations. So please take my advice as what it is – a personal view borne of many happy years of experience. How you ultimately choose to manoeuvre is up to you.

To help you absorb the information, I have attached a small self-test to each chapter. You will see that I have asked the questions, but not given you the answers – I would much prefer you to reference your answers to the Rules themselves (Chapter 12) so that you get the wording absolutely right – as so often in laws or rules, the use of specific words (for instance the difference between *'will'* and *'may'*) is absolutely critical. I suggest that you complete each test before moving onto the next chapter.

But you should also test yourself on a regular basis: find a way of engaging in gentle Rule of the Road quizzes with colleagues without making it a big issue. It needn't be dull or intrusive, and it is hugely valuable. To help with this process, I have set out a Rule of the Road test on the Wiley website (**www.wileynautical.com/colregs**).

And a word of caution . . .

Even when ships are showing the proper shapes and lights in the right place, they are not always as conspicuous or as simple as a Rule of the Road book would lead you to imagine. Large ships at anchor, for instance, often dwarf the anchor ball on their bows; fishing boat lights are often far less prominent that their working lights; and cruise liners are normally lit up like Christmas trees. You may also find that warships' navigation lights are displaced from the 'normal' position and most navies will use private flag-hoists, lights and shapes when communicating amongst themselves.

There really is no substitute for experience – hands-on experience in the bridge, wheelhouse or cockpit of a seagoing vessel – at sea and doing the business.

A vessel at anchor showing a black anchor ball.

2 Context of the Rules: *Rules 1–7*

Read through Rules 1–7 at the back of this book, before you start on this chapter.

Rules 1–7 contain some useful points about the application of the Collision Regulations that you should be familiar with.

Applicability of the Rules (Rules 1–3)

I can confidently predict that just about any competent rule-of-the-road test that you ever do will ask you where, and to whom, the Rules apply. The answer appears in Rules 1(a) and (b), and 3(a):

Rule 1

(a) These Rules shall apply to all vessels upon the high seas and in all waters connected therewith navigable by seagoing vessels.

(b) Nothing in these Rules shall interfere in the operation of special rules made by an appropriate authority for roadsteads, harbours, rivers, lakes or inland waterways connected with the high seas and navigable by seagoing vessels. Such special rules shall conform as closely as possible to these Rules.

Rule 3

(a) The word 'vessel' includes every description of watercraft, including non-displacement craft, WIG craft and seaplanes, used or capable of being used as a means of transportation on water.

The Rules apply to anything that you can think of that is **used for transport on the water**, from a raft to a super-tanker. Their jurisdiction starts at sea and extends to any inland waterway that seagoing vessels can access, unless superseded by local rules. Even so, local rules should be as close as possible to the International Rules (*Rule 1(b)*).

The Rules are actively policed in much of the world. Whether at sea or in an inland waterway, the International Maritime Organization (IMO), member states and competent local authorities have real, enactable powers to enforce compliance and to penalise those who do not comply. Ignorance or foolishness are not excuses for putting peoples' lives at risk and anyone who sets out on the water in a vessel is expected to behave responsibly. The Royal Navy administers the waters of the Eastern Solent and every year it is forced to take action against a number of individuals, driving a wide range of vessels, who behave irresponsibly in this narrow and congested waterway.

Rules 1(c) and 1(e)[1] are useful to tuck away. Governments reserve the right to authorise special shapes, signals and lights for particular vessels or functions as they see fit, provided that they can't be mistaken for any signals authorised by the Rules and that they conform as closely as possible to the sort of signals that you and I are expecting to see.

Rule 2 is all about responsibility:

> **Rule 2(a)**
>
> Nothing in these Rules shall exonerate and vessel, or the owner, master or crew thereof, from the consequences of any neglect to comply with these Rules . . .

You *must* know the Rules – and you must abide by them. You are, of course, expected to take any necessary precaution that good seamanship or 'the ordinary practice of seamen' would demand, even if those actions are not specifically prescribed in the Rules.[2] Rule 2(b) exceptionally allows experienced mariners to act outside the Rules where it is necessary 'to avoid immediate danger'.

General Definitions (Rule 3)

Don't be put off by the rather bureaucratic nature of the definitions in Rule 3: they are well worth a read and, as always, the important part lies in the small print. To pick out a few:

Rule 3(d). You don't count as a vessel engaged in fishing merely because the chef has thrown a line with a spinner over the stern. 'Engaged in fishing', under the Rules, implies two things: firstly, that you are actually fishing, and secondly that the equipment that you are using for fishing **restricts the manoeuvrability of the vessel**.

Rule 3(f). To qualify as a vessel Not Under Command (NUC), you must, **through some exceptional circumstance**, be unable to manoeuvre appropriately for collision avoidance. This is seldom premeditated, and a vessel will only declare itself Not Under Command if it is virtually powerless to take avoiding action. In other words, there is a major crisis onboard. It may still be making way, but its actions will be unpredictable and there will be a fair number of people on the bridge and elsewhere trying to sort the problem out. Keep clear. Do note, though, that the use of NUC lights or shapes is **not** a distress signal.

Rule 3(g). Six pretty disparate categories of vessel are set out in Rule 3(g): each is recognised as a vessel Restricted in her Ability to Manoeuvre (RAM). The thing that matters here is that a vessel classified as Restricted in her Ability to Manoeuvre is limited *by the nature of its work* – unlike a vessel that is Not Under Command – and this is almost always premeditated. You should always

---

[1]You will find all the Rules set out in chapter 12. Only the most significant are duplicated in the text.

[2]Failure to keep an adequate anchor watch, for instance, and dragging into another vessel could be construed as 'the neglect of any precaution which may be required by the ordinary practice of seamen'.

give these vessels space. As a naval officer, I have engaged in just about all of the Restricted in Ability to Manoeuvre activities, and there is nothing worse than knowing, for instance, that there is a diver under the water as a motor boat screams past at high speed, out of sheer curiosity and completely oblivious to the danger. Vessels restricted in their ability to manoeuvre may be more manoeuvrable than vessels not under command, but don't count on it. And occasionally, as when launching and recovering aircraft, these ships may be moving pretty fast.

2

Rule 3(g)

The term 'vessel restricted in her ability to manoeuvre' means a vessel which from the nature of her work is restricted in her ability to manoeuvre as required by these Rules and is therefore unable to keep out of the way of another vessel.

The term 'vessel restricted in her ability to manoeuvre' shall include but not be limited to:

(i)   A vessel engaged in laying, servicing, or picking up a navigational mark, submarine cable or pipeline;

(ii) A vessel engaged in dredging, surveying or underwater operations;

(iii) A vessel engaged in replenishment or transferring persons, provisions or cargo while underway;

(iv) A vessel engaged in the launching or recovery of aircraft;

(v)   A vessel engaged in mine clearance operations;

(vi) A vessel engaged in a towing operation such as severely restricts the towing vessel and her tow in their ability to deviate from their course.

Rule 3(k) and (l). Don't overlook these two rules that deal with **restricted visibility**. They are actually pretty important.

The early part of the Rules are divided into three categories:

- **Rules 4–10** apply in any condition of visibility.
- **Rules 11–18** apply when vessels are **in sight of each other**.
- **Rule 19** applies when vessels are **operating in restricted visibility**.

Annoyingly (but deliberately), 'in sight of each other' and 'operating in restricted visibility' are not quite mutually exclusive. But the point to remember is that if you can't see the other guy, for whatever reason – poor visibility, smoke, sand or some other obstruction – your rule-set is different. At times, this can be quite exciting: in patchy visibility, or on the edge of a fog bank, you may be working the 'in sight of each other' rules for one contact and the 'restricted visibility rules' for another. But there again, seafaring just wouldn't be so much fun if it was too easy!

Rule 3(k), 3(l)

(k)   Vessels shall be deemed to be in sight of one another only when one can be observed visually from the other.

(l)   The term 'restricted visibility' means any condition in which visibility is restricted by fog, mist, falling snow, heavy rainstorms, sandstorms and any other similar causes.

Proper Lookout (Rule 5)

Rule 5

Every vessel shall at all times maintain a proper look-out by sight and hearing as well as by all available means appropriate in the prevailing circumstances and conditions so as to make a full appraisal of the situation and of the risk of collision.

Keeping a good lookout is absolutely fundamental in any condition of visibility, yet most ships and most mariners are guilty of letting it slip from time to time. In a dived submarine at periscope depth and with good visibility, you scan the horizon every three minutes – less if the visibility reduces. Next time you are on watch in your yacht or your super-tanker, just ask yourself how thorough your lookout actually is – especially astern. How often do you look over your shoulder before altering course, for instance? You need to supplement a visual lookout with any other tools that you have available: radar, ARPA and AIS[3], for instance, and Vessel Traffic Services (VTS) operated by a Port Authority. In poor visibility, you may want to have someone permanently manning the radar, and to establish additional lookouts (whose job, of course, is both to look and to listen).

Safe Speed (Rule 6)

All ships react differently, but a mariner is expected to be able to gauge the **safe speed** for his ship in any given set of conditions. The speed, that is, beyond which he cannot be confident that he is **able to take proper and effective action to avoid a collision** and **to be stopped within a distance appropriate to the prevailing circumstances and conditions.** This is a particular issue in congested waters and reduced visibility. Rule 6 sets out a number of factors that affect safe speed, but there is nothing here that a relatively experienced car driver would find unusual. The parameters of visibility, traffic density, handling characteristics and all the rest are no more exotic than the decisions that you make every day on the road. In a ship or a yacht, an experienced and sensible operator will instinctively choose the right speed for any given set of conditions, and will know when he or she is going too fast.

The 12 factors for determining safe speed are important. Not only do they form a good checklist in poor visibility, but I have yet to see a rule-of-the-road test that doesn't invite you to list some or all of these factors.

---

[3]Automatic Radar Plotting Aid and Automatic Identification System.

Rule 6

Every vessel shall at all times proceed at a safe speed so that she can take proper and effective action to avoid collision and be stopped within a distance appropriate to the prevailing circumstances and conditions.

In determining a safe speed the following factors shall be among those taken into account:

(a) By all vessels:
 (i) The state of visibility;
 (ii) The traffic density including concentrations of fishing vessels or any other vessels;
 (iii) The manoeuvrability of the vessel with special reference to stopping distance and turning ability in the prevailing conditions;
 (iv) At night the presence of background light such as from shore lights or from back scatter from her own lights.
 (v) The state of wind, sea and current, and the proximity of navigational hazards;
 (vi) The draft in relation to the available depth of water.

(b) Additionally, by vessels with operational radar:
 (i) The characteristics, efficiency and limitations of the radar equipment;
 (ii) Any constrains imposed by the radar range scale in use;
 (iii) The effect on radar detection of the sea state, weather and other sources of interference;
 (iv) The possibility that small vessels, ice and other floating objects may not be detected by radar at an adequate range;
 (v) The number location and movement of vessels detected by radar;
 (vi) The more exact assessment of the visibility that may be possible when radar is used to determine the range of vessels or other objects in the vicinity.

Risk of Collision (Rule 7)

A mariner's most important skill is the ability to work out whether risk of collision exists. And the second most important skill is then to avoid the collision. We will deal with collision avoidance later, but assessing risk of collision is pretty simple:

> **Risk of collision exists when you are closing another vessel on a steady or near-steady bearing (Rule 7d).**

If the bearing doesn't alter as the range closes, you will eventually hit each other. This refers to the **compass bearing** (true or magnetic) of an approaching contact, **not the relative bearing.**

You need to start watching the bearing of approaching vessels while they are still quite distant. Initially, no matter how good your equipment, the bearing will appear to be relatively steady. At some point though, and this is a matter of judgment, you will expect to see evidence of sustained and accelerating bearing movement. If the bearing remains steady, you must consider what action to take, but even if there is bearing movement, you should still keep a beady eye on it (it might suddenly change course or speed and steady the bearing up again). So never assume that another vessel is safe without systematically checking its bearing. In the words of Rule 7(a): 'If there is any doubt, such risk [of collision] shall be deemed to exist.'

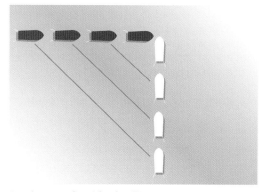

Bearing steady: risk of collision exists.

Even when you are systematically taking bearings, and they are moving, you still need to exercise caution. A few years ago on passage through the Straits of Dover, I was diligently taking bearings of the stern of an adjacent ship that was passing at close range, watching it move steadily left. It was only when I got really close that I realised that, while the stern was still moving left, the bow had started to move right. Somewhere in between, my logic told me, there must be

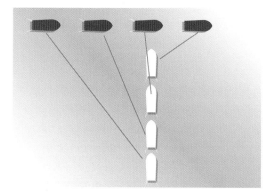

Bearing drawing steadily right: no risk of collision.

a part of the ship that was on a steady bearing and, if I didn't take some fairly rapid action we would collide. At close quarters, or with long vessels or tows, you need to make sure that all parts are moving in the same relative direction (Rule 7(d)(ii)).

Rule 7d

In determining if risk of collision exists the following considerations shall be among those taken into account:

(i)   Such risk shall be deemed to exist if the compass bearing of an approaching vessel does not appreciably change;

(ii)   Such risk may sometimes exist even when an appreciable bearing change is evident, particularly when approaching a very large vessel or a tow or when approaching a vessel at close range.

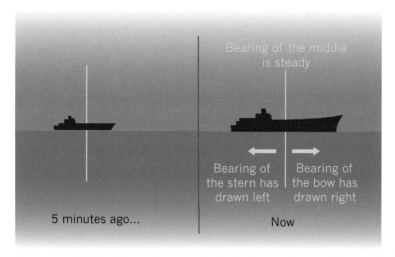

Bearing of the middle
is steady

Bearing of
the stern has
drawn left

Bearing of
the bow has
drawn right

5 minutes ago...

Now

2

Be very careful when close to large vessels; the bearing of all parts of the vessel, and anything that it is towing, must be moving in the same direction.

So whenever you see another vessel that might pose a threat, check whether its **compass bearing** is steady or moving, and continue to check it until it is past. In a big ship with a stabilised gyro compass, it is generally quite easy to get regular and accurate bearings, but in a yacht or a fishing vessel, bouncing around in a heavy swell, this is something of an art form. **But even if it is difficult, you must *always* check the bearing movement of an approaching contact.**

Quite a useful technique is to check the other ship's movement against the background.[4] In general, you can consider the background, if sufficiently distant, to be on a more-or-less steady bearing. Watch the other vessel and see if it moves against this backdrop: it will either be moving right, left or remain steady, and this will be a pretty good indicator of its bearing movement. Don't take this as gospel truth, though: it is merely an indicator. Clouds drift across the sky, land will probably have a gentle bearing movement one way or another as you move past it, so you will need to take this into account. However, if you are sensible, you may well find this a useful way of routinely checking other vessels' bearing movement – and helping you decide which ones you need to concentrate on.

---

[4]In a different context, you do this every day. Each time you cross a road, or walk through a busy station concourse you subconsciously judge the danger of collision by watching the movement of oncoming cars or people against the background.

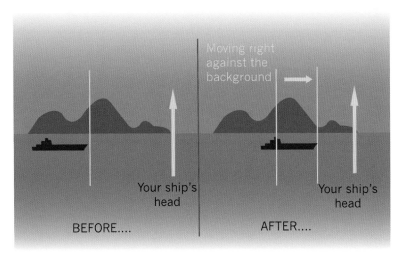

Bearing of the vessel is probably moving right: likely to pass ahead.

You may be tempted to check bearing movement by reference to a fixed part of the ship's structure like a crane, a bridge window or a guardrail stanchion. This gives you a *relative bearing*, and your ability to tell whether the **compass bearing** is steady or not will depend absolutely on the ship's directional stability, and whether you stand in the same place each time you check. Use it if you find it helpful, but with great care. Personally, I have never found it particularly reliable and I wouldn't recommend it.

In summary, there are three important issues contained in Rule 7:

- Firstly, a risk of collision exists if the compass bearing is steady. Even if the bearing is moving, however, there may still be a risk of collision, particularly when working close to a long vessel or tow.

- Secondly, use all available information to assess risk of collision and, if you are in any doubt, assume that a risk of collision *does* exist until you prove otherwise.

- And thirdly, don't be seduced to make assumptions based on scanty information, especially scanty radar information. If you don't have enough information, keep your options open until you know more.

'Under Way' and 'Making Way' (Rule 3i)

It is crucial that you understand the difference between the terms: **under way** and **making way**.

- **Under way** is defined in Rule 3(i): it refers to any vessel that is not secured to a fixed object; a vessel, in other words, that 'is not at anchor, or made fast to the shore, or aground.'
- **'Making way'** is not specifically defined in the Rules, but it refers to any vessel that is moving through the water.

To make way, therefore, you must be under way. If, however, you are stopped and drifting, you would be under way, but not making way.

This raises a good question to while away the slow night watches: are you under way, making way or at anchor when your anchor is dragging? The answer is that you are under way, not making way, and as a result you still have a responsibility for collision avoidance.

2

Chapter 2 – Self-test (Rules 1–7)

2

1. Where do these Rules apply? (*Rule 1(a)*.)

2. In the event that a harbour has its own particular rules, do those rules have precedence over the Collision Regulations, or not? (*Rule 1(b)*.)

3. Complete the following rules:

    a. 3(a): *The word 'vessel' includes every description of _____ _____, including non-displacement craft, WIG craft and seaplanes, _____ or capable of being _____ as a means of _____ ____ _____.'*

    b. 3(b): *The term 'power-driven vessel' means any vessel _____ ____ _____.*

    c. 3(d): *The term 'vessel engaged in fishing' means any vessel fishing with nets, lines trawls or other fishing apparatus which _____, but does not include a vessel fishing with trolling lines or other fishing apparatus which ____ ____ _____ _____.*

4. There are six categories of vessel which are Restricted in their Ability to Manoeuvre. Can you name them? (*Rule 3(g)*.)

5. What do the terms 'under way' and 'making way' mean? (*Rule 3(i)*.)

6. Complete Rule 5:

    Every vessel shall at all times maintain a proper lookout by sight _____ as well as by ____ _____ _____ _____ to the prevailing circumstances and conditions so as to make a _____ _____ of the situation and the Risk of Collision.

7. The first sentence of Rule 6 instructs mariners to maintain a safe speed at all times so that they can carry out two specific actions. Can you name them?

8. The inevitable question: name as many of the factors for determining safe speed as you can. There are 12 in all. Six apply to 'all vessels', and the second six apply in restricted visibility. (*Rule 6(a) and (b)*.)

9. If you are in any doubt whether a risk of collision exists, what must you assume? (*Rule 7(a)*.)

10. What is the principal means for determining whether a risk of collision exists? (*Rule 7(d)(i)*.)

3 How to Recognise other Vessels by their Lights and Shapes: *Rules 20–31 and 36*

Read through Rules 20–31 and 36 before you start on this chapter.

Vessels carry lights and shapes for two purposes:

1   To establish the presence and orientation of the ship, and whether it is under way and making way. This is done with side, stern and masthead lights which I will refer to as **navigation lights**.

2   To establish how manoeuvrable a ship is in comparison to others. This is done with supplementary lights and shapes that I will refer to as **identification lights and shapes**.

The Rules assume that power-driven vessels have complete freedom of movement (unless they are Not Under Command (**NUC**); Restricted in their Ability to Manoeuvre (RAM), and so on). Every other vessel is, by implication, constrained to a greater or lesser extent in its ability to avoid a collision. We will come to the Manoeuvring Rules in Chapter 5, and we will see that Rule 18 establishes a 'hierarchy' that requires more manoeuvrable vessels to keep out of the way of those that are less manoeuvrable. For this to work, the ships that are less manoeuvrable must make sure that they clearly signal their limitations – by lights, shapes and sound signals.

Unencumbered power-driven vessels do not carry identification lights or shapes, but any vessel with a manoeuvring limitation does.

If possible, you should always check the other vessel's lights and shapes before deciding on any avoiding action, in order to determine its orientation and where it stands on the manoeuvring hierarchy.

In daylight and good visibility, it is relatively easy to identify another vessel by eye, and to calculate its approximate range and orientation. A fishing boat is pretty much unmistakable, for instance, as is a dredger. But a vessel's manoeuvrability is often less easy to work out, and that's what the shapes are for. For instance:

■   Are those two merchant vessels following closely behind each other doing so by chance – or is one towing the other?

■   Is that sailing vessel using its engine for propulsion, or is it just sailing?

■ What about that container ship coming up the narrow channel – is it free to manoeuvre, or is it constrained by its draught?

At night, or in restricted visibility, just about every vessel will show **sidelights** and a **sternlight**. In addition, the majority will show one or two **masthead lights**. These lights, taken as a whole, are invaluable; to an experienced eye, they will tell you what sort of ship it is, together with its range and orientation and likely size.[1] But they won't tell you how manoeuvrable it is. For this, you need to check for any identification lights, which may or may not be displayed with side, stern or masthead lights, depending on the circumstances.

When Lights and Shapes Must be Used (Rule 20)

Rule 20

(a) Rules in this part shall be complied with in all weathers.

(b) The Rules concerning lights shall be complied with from sunset to sunrise, and during such times no other lights shall be exhibited, except such lights which cannot be mistaken for the lights specified in these Rules or do not impair their visibility or distinctive character, or interfere with the keeping of a proper look-out.

(c) The lights prescribed by these rules shall, if carried, also be exhibited from sunrise to sunset in restricted visibility and may be exhibited in all other circumstances when it is deemed necessary.

(d) The Rules concerning shapes shall be complied with by day.

(e) The lights and shapes specified in these Rules shall comply with the provisions of Annex I to these Regulations.

Lights are to be shown on three specific occasions are:

■ **From sunset to sunrise**

■ **In restricted visibility**, by day or night

■ And **whenever the Master considers it necessary**.

Shapes are to be shown by day. They should remain hoisted after sunset and before sunrise, so long as they can be seen by other seafarers. During twilight, therefore, you should show both shapes and lights.

---

[1]Do remember that lights and shapes are always exaggerated in books like this. Real life is seldom so simple: lights will frequently be much more difficult to see, or lost against the background. Shapes may simply be wooded by the ship's superstructure.

NAVIGATION LIGHTS

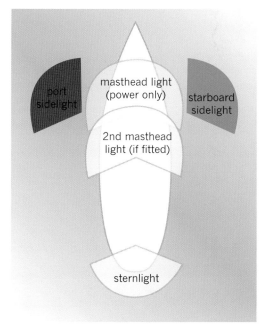

All lights cut off 22½° abaft the beam.

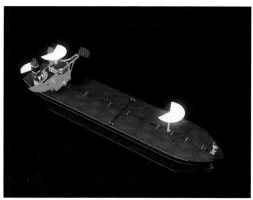

A power driven vessel under way, showing side lights, sternlight and 2 masthead lights.

Side and Sternlights (Rule 21)

Side and sternlights, between them, cover the full 360 degrees of arc. Their purpose is to let you know that there is a vessel there and allow you to estimate its orientation[2]. Side and sternlights (unlike the masthead lights) are displayed by very nearly all vessels under way at night or in restricted visibility, with only a very few exceptions[3].

The port (red) and starboard (green)[4] bow lights extend from the bow to the cut-in of the sternlight, 22.5 degrees abaft the respective beam, and the sternlight covers the stern sector, from 22.5 degrees abaft one beam, through the stern to the same angle on the other side.

There is no clever way of remembering 22.5 degrees, but it is an important angle because the Rules also stipulate that any vessel closing from within the arc of the sternlight, by day or night, is an **overtaking vessel**, with all the obligations that that brings (Rule 13b).

---

[2]Lights are profoundly important: it is well worth checking your own navigation lights each evening before sunset: check they work, check that they are not fouled by obstructions and, when you can, check that the cut-offs are as sharp as possible and there is minimal cross-over. For yachtsmen, make sure that you know which switches to make when you are sailing and when you are motoring. Setting the wrong lights makes you look shabby, and it can be profoundly confusing for other mariners.

[3]Vessels Not Under Command; Restricted in their Ability to Manoeuvre, and Engaged in Fishing show side and sternlights only when making way.

[4]'Left' has four letters, as does 'port' – which is of course a red-coloured wine, like the port sidelight.

Masthead Lights (Rule 21)

Masthead lights are white lights carried at, or close to the masthead with arcs of visibility extending through the bow to an angle of 22.5 degrees abaft each beam. This is, of course, the arc of the two sidelights combined.

Power-driven vessels will generally carry two masthead lights, the after one discernibly higher than the forward one. If, however, the vessel is shorter than 50 metres in length, it *may* show only one masthead light.

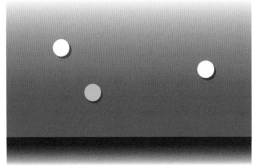

Power driven vessel, viewed from broad on starboard side – could be any length.

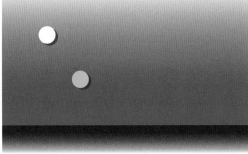

Power driven vessel, viewed from the starboard side – less than 50m in length.

Masthead lights are shown by nearly all power-driven vessels under way. They are also shown by sailing vessels operating under power, but not when sailing.

There are only a few types of power-driven vessels that don't show masthead lights: Vessels Not Under Command, pilot vessels, and fishing boats Engaged in Fishing (although trawlers greater than 50 metres in length do).

IDENTIFICATION LIGHTS

Sidelights, the sternlight and masthead lights are all sectored. Identification lights, on the other hand, are generally visible around 360 degrees of horizon[5] so that anyone approaching from any angle can see what is going on and decide what action to take. Identification lights are usually located below the masthead lights and above the side and sternlights.

---

[5]Towing lights are the only exception to this.

3

How to identify vessels at night

Most people find the reading of ships' lights confusing when they start. My advice would be always to begin with the sidelights or sternlight, and the masthead lights: these are *single* white, red or green lights, which will be in a fairly predictable layout, depending on the size and aspect of the ship. Once you have sorted this out, look (normally below the masthead lights) for any identification lights to tell you what the vessel is doing.

Take your time and go about it logically. It's not simple, but most vessels do actually show the prescribed lights and shapes, even if they are not always easy to pick out. Even experienced mariners get confused sometimes: I once spent a whole hour looking through a submarine's periscope on a dark night, taking bearings of a single white light that was slowly rising above the horizon, utterly convinced that it was a power-driven vessel closing me on a steady bearing. To my great embarrassment, and to the great amusement of my colleagues, it turned out to be Venus.

On the right is a pretty extreme case of complex navigation lights: it shows a power-driven vessel, less than 50 metres in length, viewed from the starboard side. The vessel is Restricted in its Ability to Manoeuvre, and dredging or conducting underwater operations. It would be dangerous to pass down its starboard side.

Now look at the identification process:

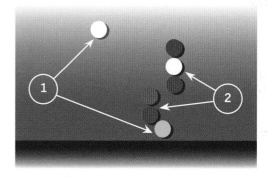

Lights can be confusing.

1. One single (white) masthead light and a single (green) sidelight show that it is a power-driven vessel, less than 50 metres in length, viewed from the starboard side.

2. The identification lights (red-white-red and red-over-red) give you all the rest of the information, which is just a matter of learning the meaning of various light combinations.

LIGHTS AND SHAPES

I will divide the next section into four parts:

1. **The most familiar lights:** the ones carried by vessels that are least impaired in their ability to manoeuvre (power-driven vessels, tows, pilot vessels and fishing vessels).

2. **The more constrained categories of vessel:** Restricted in their Ability to Manoeuvre or Not Under Command.

3. **Those vessels that simply cannot manoeuvre at all:** anchored and aground.

4. **A few oddballs:** ones that you might see from time to time, and should certainly be able to recognise when you do.

Part 1: The Most Familiar Lights

Power-driven vessels under way (Rule 23)

Definition:

3

Rule 3(b)

■ The term 'power-driven vessel' means any vessel propelled by machinery.

Rule 3(i)

■ The word 'under way' means that a vessel is not at anchor, or made fast to the shore, or aground.

Shapes: None

Identification lights: None

Side and sternlights: Yes: when under way.

Masthead lights:

■ Yes, when under way.

■ Two masthead lights, the after one higher than the forward light

■ Vessels less than 50m in length may show just one masthead light.

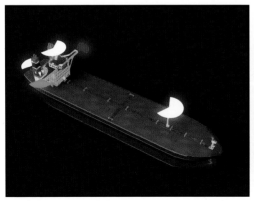

A power driven vessel, under way.

A power driven vessel, less than 50m in length, under way.

3

Small vessels:

- A vessel of less than 12 metres in length may, instead of the above lights, show an all-round white light and sidelights.

- A vessel of less than 7 metres in length whose speed does not exceed 7 knots may, instead of the above lights, show a white all-round light. Additional sidelights are recommended but not obligatory.

A power driven vessel less than 12 metres in length.

A power driven vessel less than 7 metres in length and capable of less than 7 knots.

Notes:

- These lights are shown whether a vessel is making way or not – provided that she is under way (that is, not at anchor, made fast to the shore or aground). In other words, they are shown whenever the vessel is capable of taking action to avoid a collision.

- A second masthead light is optional for vessels less than 50 metres in length.

- A sailing vessel operating her engine – whether she has sails raised or not – is expected to manoeuvre as an unencumbered power-driven vessel.

- Specific lights and shapes for Wing-In-Ground craft, air cushion vessels and submarines, all of which are power-driven vessels, are covered at the end of this chapter.

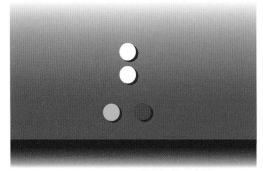

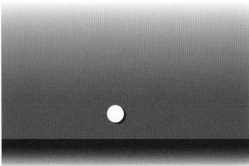

Power driven vessel, viewed from right ahead.

Power driven vessel, viewed from within the sector of the sternlight.

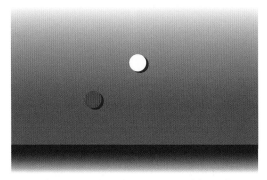

Power driven vessel, under way, viewed from the port side. The vessel is less than 50m in length.

Sailing Vessels (Rule 25)

Definition:

Rule 3(c)

The term 'sailing vessel' means any vessel under sail provided that propelling machinery, if fitted, is not being used.

Shapes:

- None when just sailing.
- When the engine is being used as well as sails, a cone apex downward is shown forward where it can best be seen. This is not necessary if *only* propelling by machinery – that is, if all the sails are furled.

A sailing vessel using her engines for propulsion, but with sails hoisted.

Identification lights: A red all-round light over a green all-round light at the masthead is optional for sailing vessels[6].

Side and sternlights:

- Sidelights and sternlights are shown when under way, even when stopped in the water.

- Sailing vessels less than 20 metres in length can amalgamate these three lights into a single combined lantern with the same colours over the same arcs. This is shown at the masthead, but *not* when the engine is being used for propulsion, when the boat shows lights for a power-driven vessel, and the masthead light is separate from the sidelights.

- Sailing vessels less than 7 metres in length should show side and sternlights if they can. If not, they should have a white torch of sufficient strength to help it avoid a collision.

Masthead lights:

- None when sailing.

- When the engine is being used, a single, sectored white light on or close to the masthead.(This may be an all-round light if the vessel is less than 12 metres in length (*Rule 23(d)(i)*).

---

[6]I remember this as the same alignment as traffic lights – red over green.

3

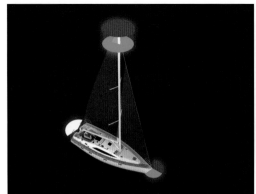

Sailing vessel underway.

A sailing vessel, under way and sailing.

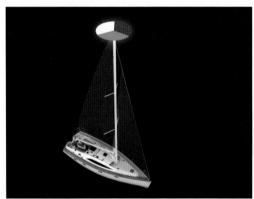

A sailing vessel less than 20 metres in length, using a combined masthead lantern.

A sailing vessel less than 50 metres in length propelling itself by power.

Notes:

■ Only a very few sailing boats – normally the larger ones – carry the two all-round red-over-green lights at the masthead. Understandably, it should not be used when a combined lantern is shown at the masthead.

■ Most sailing boats make do with sidelights and a sternlight when sailing and the majority of yachtsmen (that is, those with boats less than 20 metres in length) combine them into a single sectored lantern at the masthead.

■ A combined lantern is relatively easy to spot from ahead: no other vessel shows just a single red or green light at the masthead. From astern – a single white light – it is a little more ambiguous.

- From the bridge of a ship, yachts are never easy to pick up, particularly at night, and especially against a background of shore lights. Their lights are weaker than other vessels, and surprisingly often they are partially obstructed (life rafts and guardrails are prime culprits). They may also sometimes by wooded by sails or the boat's movement.

- When a sailing boat starts using its engines for propulsion, it must change over to the proper steaming lights. I have frequently seen a combined lantern at the masthead and a white steaming light, below it, half-way down the mast. This is both sloppy and confusing.

3

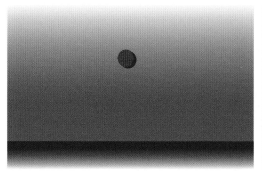

Sailing vessel less than 20 metres in length, seen from her port side. (Using a combined masthead lantern.)

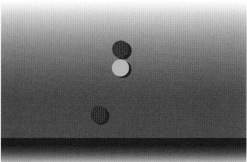

Sailing vessel, seen from the port side.

Fishing Vessels – Trawling (Rule 26)

Definitions

- The Rules specify two distinct types of fishing vessel – trawlers and 'vessels engaged in fishing other than trawling'. They carry almost identical shapes, but the lights are very different.

Rule 3(d)

- The term vessel **Engaged in Fishing** means any vessel fishing with nets, lines, trawls, or other fishing apparatus which restrict manoeuvrability, but does not include a vessel fishing with trolling lines or other fishing apparatus which do not restrict manoeuvrability.

Rule 26(b)

- A vessel when engaged in trawling, by which is meant the dragging through the water of a dredge net or other apparatus used as a fishing appliance. . . .

3

Shapes: Two cones, apex together, in a vertical line one above the other.

Identification lights: Green all-round light above a white all-round light. At all times when trawling.

Side and sternlights: Side and sternlights, but **only when making way**.

Masthead lights:

- For vessels greater than 50 metres in length, a masthead light mounted higher than and abaft the two identification lights when trawling.

- For vessels less than 50 metres in length, the masthead light is optional.

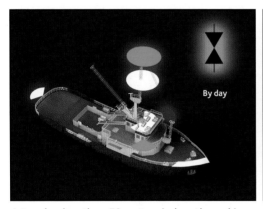

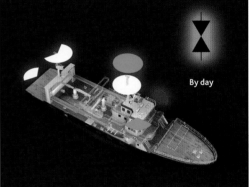

A trawler, less than 50 metres in length, making way.

A trawler, possibly greater than 50 metres in length, making way.

Notes:

- The identification lights and a masthead light are to be shown (Rule 26a) when the vessel is engaged in fishing, whether underway or at anchor. And the side and sternlights are only shown when making way. In practice, however, trawling normally requires the vessel to be both under way and making way, so this is all a little academic.

- Trawlers are the most common type of fishing vessel that you will see in Northern European waters. Like most fishing boats, their navigation lights will be eclipsed by working lights – great white arc lights that are used to floodlight the deck at night, and which are quite unmistakable from a distance.

- Give trawlers as much clearance as you can: when hauling their catch, their gear can often lie on the surface up to 150 metres astern.

- Try to go round a fishing fleet if possible, but if you find yourself in the middle of one – and this generally happens at 0330 in the morning – look for the path of least resistance and take it one boat at a time. They are not going to be moving very fast so just make sure that you get a positive bearing movement on anything that looks close.

- There are some pretty arcane rules for trawlers and purse seiners working in close proximity to one another that are set out in Annex II of the Rules. Frankly, I have only seen them infrequently, but they are used, and the main purpose of these signals is to communicate with other fishing vessels. For completeness, the working light signals are as follows:

  - When shooting nets   Two white lights in a vertical line
  - When hauling in their nets   White over red all-round light
  - When nets caught on an obstruction   Two red lights in a vertical line

- Vessels engaged in 'pair trawling' (when 2 boats work together with a single trawl, one pulling each side of the net) at night may have a searchlight directed towards the direction of the other vessel to stop anyone from cutting between the boats.

- Vessels engaged in 'purse seining' (where a single fishing vessel sets out a net in a circle, joins both ends and closes the bottom to form the shape of a 'purse') may show two vertically displaced yellow lights, flashing alternately.

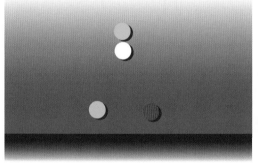

Trawler, less than 50 metres in length, making way and seen from ahead.

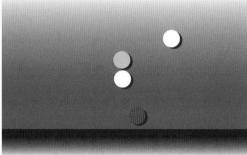

Trawler, possibly greater than 50 metres in length, making way, and seen from the port side.

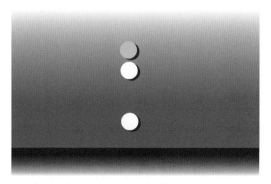

Trawler, making way and seen from astern.

Fishing Vessels – Other than Trawling (Rule 26)

Definition:

3

Rule 3(d)

The term 'Vessel Engaged in Fishing' means any vessel fishing with nets, lines, trawls, or other fishing apparatus which restrict manoeuvrability, but does not include a vessel fishing with trolling lines or other fishing apparatus which do not restrict manoeuvrability.

Shapes:

- Two cones, apex together in a vertical line one above the other.
- A single cone, apex upwards, in the direction of outlying gear when that gear extends more than 150 metres away from the boat.

Identification lights:

- A red all-round light above a white all-round light
- White all-round light in the direction of the outlying gear, if it extends more than 150 metres from the boat.

Side and sternlightsternlights:

- Sidelights and sternlights **only when making way through the water**

Masthead lights: None when fishing.

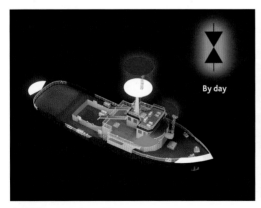

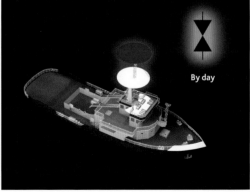

A fishing vessel, making way.   *A fishing vessel, stopped in the water.*

Notes:

- There are two criteria for being a **vessel engaged in fishing**: you have to be fishing, and your fishing gear must impede your ability to manoeuvre.
- Fishing boats, other than trawlers, do not show a steaming light at the masthead when fishing. When stopped in the water (that is, under way, but not making way), neither shows side or sternlights.
- In practice, a fishing vessel's working lights normally outshine any identification lights that it might be showing. You should, however, be able to see the appropriate lights.
- By day, there is no mistaking a fishing vessel, and in practice most of them leave the shapes hoisted whether they are fishing or not. You will often see boats tied up in harbour with their cones still up, and occasionally with their fishing lights still switched on too. But if you see the upward pointing cone, indicating outlying gear, you do need to pay attention, and give it a good clearance.
- When not engaged in fishing, all fishing vessels show the lights and shapes, as appropriate, of a power-driven vessel.
- The keen-eyed amongst you will spot that there is scope for confusion between the lights of a fishing vessel **not making way** with outlying gear extending more than 150 metres, and the same vessel **making way**, seen from the arc of the sternlight. I doubt if this will be a problem in practice.

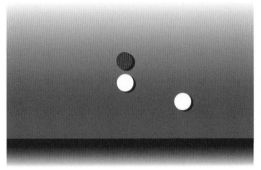 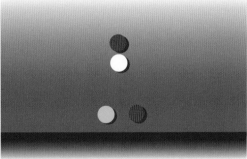

Fishing vessel, stopped in the water, with gear outlying more than 150 metres in the direction of the white light.

Fishing vessel making way, viewed from right ahead.

Pilot Vessels (Rule 29)

Definition: None. Only applies to vessels actually engaged on pilotage duty.

Shapes: None.

Identification lights: White all-round light over a red all-round light at the masthead when engaged on pilotage duty.

3

Side and sternlights: Side and sternlights when under way.

Masthead lights: None when engaged on pilotage duty: the white and red lights are shown at the masthead.

Anchor lights: Anchor lights appropriate to the length of the vessel are shown together with the pilot identification lights when at anchor on pilotage duty.

A pilot vessel under way.

A pilot vessel, by day – pretty unmistakeable.

Notes:

- This is one of a very small number of power-driven vessels that don't show masthead lights when under way.

- Although no shapes are prescribed in the Rules for a pilot vessel, you will seldom see one which does not have the letters 'P I L O T', or the local equivalent, painted down the side. They sometimes fly International Code flag 'H' – vertically halved white and red.(Just occasionally, too, you see a flag that is halved horizontally: a red and white flag.)

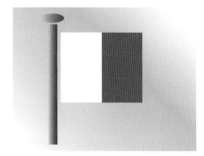

International Code: 'HOTEL'
"I have a pilot onboard."

- Don't confuse the pilot vessel lights with those of a fishing vessel. There is no similarity in the way the vessels operate. I remember the 'white-over-red' lights as a pilot's weather-beaten red nose underneath his white seaman's cap. Alternatively, you can remember a fishing vessels' lights with the little ditty: 'Red over white – frying tonight'.

- Theoretically, there is also scope for confusion between the lights of a pilot vessel less than 50 metres in length at anchor, and a pilot vessel under way seen from the arc of the sternlight. I shouldn't lose too much sleep over it!

■ Pilot boats are great enthusiasts. They are either going flat out to and from a ship, or else stopped in the water. Frequently they will loiter or anchor at the approaches to a port at the Pilot Station, which is marked on Admiralty charts with a vertical magenta diamond in a magenta circle.

3

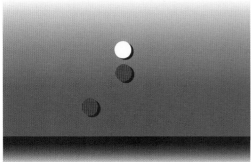
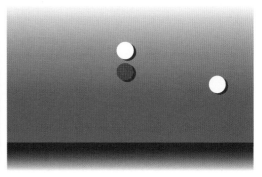

Pilot vessel on pilotage duty, under way, seen from the port side.

Pilot vessel, on pilotage duty, at anchor. Less than 50 metres in length.

Towing Vessels (Rule 24)

Definition: None.

Shapes:

■ If the tow is greater than 200 metres in length: a diamond shape where it can be best seen.

■ When the length of the tow is less than 200 metres, no signal is shown.

Identification lights:

■ Two masthead lights in a vertical line if the tow is less than 200 metres in length.

■ Three masthead lights in a vertical line if the tow is greater than 200 metres in length.

■ A yellow, sectored towing light vertically above the sternlight with the same arcs of visibility as the sternlight.(Only when towing by the stern – not when towing alongside or pushing ahead.)

Side and sternlights: Standard stern and sidelights when under way.

Masthead lights:

- The forward masthead light is replaced by two or three white identification lights which show over the same arcs as a steaming light.
- If the towing vessel is longer than 50 metres, it *must* (and a smaller vessel *may*) show a separate steaming light, abaft and higher than the forward masthead lights – as for a standard power-driven vessel.

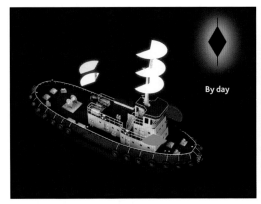

A power driven vessel, less than 50 metres in length, towing astern. Length of the tow is greater than 200 metres.

A power driven vessel, possibly greater than 50 metres in length, towing astern. Length of the tow does not exceed 200 metres.

The length of the tow is measured from the stern of the tug to the stern of the final vessel in the tow.

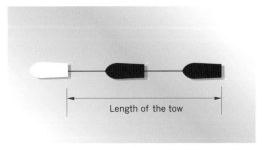

A tug and two vessels being towed. The length of the tow is measured from the stern of the tug to the stern of the final vessel in the tow.

Notes:

- This is one of the more complex sets of lights and shapes, *but* you do see tows surprisingly often. Tows are only considered to have manoeuvring limitations when they are showing restricted-in-their-ability-to-manoeuvre shapes or lights in addition to the towing signals. If RAM lights and shapes are not shown, the tow can be expected to manoeuvre as a simple power-driven vessel.

- The towing signals are there to tell you what is happening and to give you an indication of the overall length of the tow. A tow is pretty easy to pick out by eye, however, even if you can't see the towing cable, because there will be two or more vessels in line astern moving relatively slowly through the water.

- Even so, the yellow light is important by night; most vessels are going to be moving faster than a tow, and so they will be regularly overtaken. The yellow light is the only visual indication from astern at night that these vessels constitute a tow, and it is there to prevent anyone from cutting in between the towing vessel and the tow. Clearly, this is not necessary when towing alongside or pushing ahead.

- The lights are not difficult to remember. My mnemonic for the diamond shape is that, if the tow is greater than 200 metres in length it must be valuable. Therefore, both the tug and the tow show a diamonds shape in the rigging.

- You may sometimes have to take another vessel in tow, whether your vessel is designed to do so or not. Rule 24(i) exonerates vessels that are not designed for towing from showing these lights and shapes. But even so, you must make sure that you take 'all possible measures to indicate the nature of the relationship between the towing vessel and the vessel being towed': the last thing that you need is for someone to run over your towline by mistake. This is normally achieved by a searchlight playing over the towline, but check out the cautions in Rule 36 for 'Signals to Attract Attention' at the end of this chapter.

3

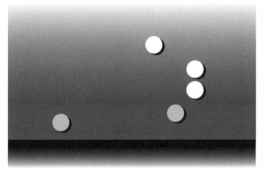

Towing vessel, possibly greater than 50 metres in length, with one vessel in the tow. Tow is less than 200 metres in length. Seen from the starboard side.

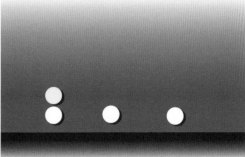

Towing vessel and 2 vessels being towed, seen from the port quarter.

Vessels Being Towed Astern (Rule 24)

Shapes:

- If the tow is greater than 200 metres in length: a diamond shape where it can be best seen. (Note that there is no equivalent light signal.)

- **A tow consisting of an inconspicuous or partly submerged object**, like flexible oil barges (also known as dracones[7]), or floats of timber, will show a diamond shape at the back end of the last vessel or object being towed. If the length of the tow exceeds 200 metres, a second diamond is showed at the front end of the vessel or object being towed (this marks the extremities of the object being towed).

A dracone. Can be up to 300 feet in length.

Identification lights:

- None for a routine tow.

- Inconspicuous or partially submerged objects being towed:

  - If it is less than 25 metres wide, one all-round white light at the front and back (for dracones, only at the back).

  - If it is 25 metres or more in breadth, two additional white lights to mark the extremities of its breadth.

  - If it is more than 100 metres in length, (in other words, a monster), additional white lights along its length at intervals not exceeding 100 metres.

Side and sternlights: Sidelights and sternlights are shown when under way, but not – for obvious reasons – on an inconspicuous or semi-submerged object being towed.

Masthead lights: None

---

[7]No, I've never seen a dracone either, nor have I heard anyone speak of them outside the context of the Rule of the Road. But they do exist and if you have the inclination, check out the Universal Rope website: www.universalrope.com/dracone.html and then try to work out how you would spot one at sea.

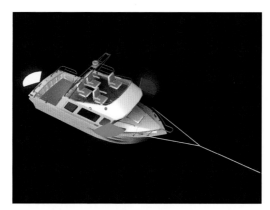

A vessel being towed. Would show a diamond by day if the tow was greater than 200 metres in length.

Notes:

I wish I could make this easier and less complicated for you.

- Ordinary vessels being towed are pretty simple; inconspicuous or partially-submerged objects are a bit more difficult – but all the Rules are doing here is staking out their extremities for other mariners to keep clear.
- In practice, unless you are in a logging area or plain unlucky, you won't come across an inconspicuous or partially submerged object being towed, and the great majority of tows that you encounter will be straightforward – with or without a diamond shape, and with simple side and sternlights. Focus on that, and memorise the rest!

Vessels Towing and Being Towed Alongside or Pushed Ahead (Rule 24)

Definition: None.

Shapes: None.

Identification lights:

- None on the vessels being towed alongside or pushed ahead.
- Tug shows two masthead lights in a vertical line (as for a vessel towing when the length of the tow is less than 200 metres, but with no towing light.)

Side and sternlights: Sidelights and sternlights for tug and the vessel being towed alongside or pushed ahead – *except* that a vessel being pushed ahead does not show a sternlight.

Masthead lights:

- The forward masthead light is replaced by two white masthead lights in a vertical line.
- If the towing vessel is longer than 50 metres, it *must* (and a smaller vessel *may*) show a separate masthead light, abaft of and higher than the masthead identification lights – as for a standard power-driven vessel.

The length of the tow is measured from the stern of the tug to the stern of the final vessel in the tow.

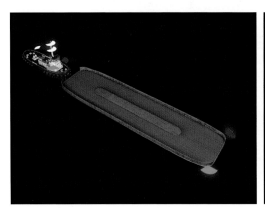 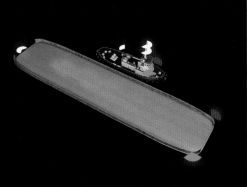

A vessel being pushed ahead, not part of a composite unit.   *A vessel being towed alongside.*

Notes:

- This form of towing is very common in harbours and sheltered waters; I have seldom seen it on the high seas.
- Vessels being towed alongside show sidelights and a sternlight. If a vessel being pushed ahead showed a sternlight, however, it would blind the bridge of the pushing vessel, so it just shows sidelights.
- The tug does not display a yellow towing light.
- No shape is shown by either vessel.
- It is not always easy to manoeuvre a unit of this nature in a restricted piece of water; although they are technically power-driven vessels, you should give them a little clearance if you can.
- **Composite Units:** Rule 24 also talks about vessels that are '. . . rigidly connected as a composite unit'. These are purpose-built tugs and barges that can lock together to form a single, bigger, power-driven vessel. Once connected, they are to all intents and purposes indistinguishable from any other power-driven vessels. They are lit, and should be treated, as such. They don't require a second thought from the rest of us.

3

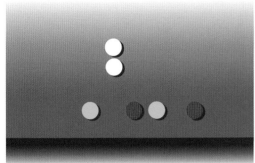

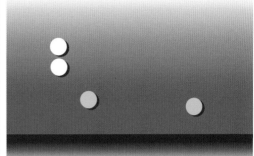

Tug towing another vessel alongside, with the tow on her port side. Tug is less than 50 metres in length. Seen from right ahead.

Tug, less than 50 metres in length, pushing another vessel ahead, seen from the starboard side.

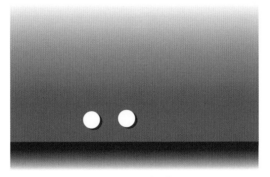

Tug and tow, towing alongside, from astern.

Part 2: Vessels that are More Constrained

That is the end of the vessels which are relatively free to manoeuvre. We will now move on to three categories of vessel that are telling you that they will have quite serious difficulty in obeying the manoeuvring rules.

Ships will display NUC shapes and lights when something has gone wrong (*some exceptional circumstance – Rule 3(f)*) that has a direct bearing on their manoeuvrability – power failure, steering gear broken, and so on.

A more premeditated category, but one that still needs to be viewed with respect, is **Restricted in Ability to Manoeuvre (RAM)** where the limitations are imposed by the employment of the ship at that time. Cable-laying is a good example, when the ship itself is perfectly serviceable, but the fact that it is connected to 2000 nautical miles of trans-Atlantic cable must to some extent limit her ability to get out of your way. There are six categories of RAM in all, three of which have distinct lights and shapes: dredgers and vessels engaged in underwater operations, vessels engaged in mine clearance operations, and vessels engaged in towing where the tow severely restricts the ability of the vessels involved to manoeuvre (tows that are not restricted in their ability to manoeuvre do not show RAM lights). I have dealt with these three separately.

Finally, don't expect a **vessel constrained by its draught** to make many concessions to other shipping: it is in a tight waterway with very limited freedoms of manoeuvre, and quite often has only limited stopping power.

Not Under Command (NUC) (Rule 27)

Definition:

> **Rule 3(f)**
> The term 'vessel Not Under Command' means a vessel which through some <u>exceptional circumstance</u> is unable to manoeuvre as required by these Rules and is therefore unable to keep out of the way of another vessel.

Shapes: Two balls in a vertical line where they can be best seen.

Identification lights: Two red all-round lights, one above the other.

Side and sternlights: Sidelights and sternlights **only when making way through the water.**

Masthead lights: None.

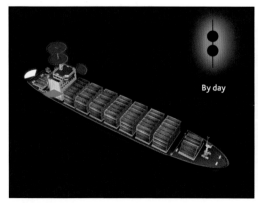

A vessel Not Under Command, making way.

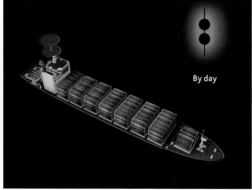

A vessel Not Under Command, under way, but not making way.

Notes:

- In the manoeuvring 'hierarchy' that we will come to in Chapter 5, vessels NUC and RAM are the least manoeuvrable. Every other vessel is instructed to keep out of their way (Rule 18).

- It is important for other mariners to get as much information as they can about a vessel Not Under Command. You can assume that it is under way, for the simple reason that its inability to manoeuvre would not be an issue if it was at anchor. But you need to know whether it is making way or not in order to help you decide how best to keep clear. If it is dead in the water, it doesn't show side and sternlights. If it is making way, it does.

- Standard masthead lights would only confuse a very clear and unambiguous signal coming from the two red all-round lights – so they are not shown at all.

- I don't know how to put this in a genteel fashion, but I have always remembered the lights and shapes of a vessel NUC on the grounds that the engineer has made a balls-up. Therefore two black balls and two red lights.

This is *not* a distress signal

Vessel Not Under Command, under way but not making way.

Vessel Not Under Command, making way, seen from the port side.

Restricted in Ability to Manoeuvre (RAM) Rule 27

Definition:

Rule 3(g)

The term 'vessel restricted in her ability to manoeuvre' means a vessel which ***from the nature of her work*** is restricted in her ability to manoeuvre as required by these Rules and is therefore unable to keep out of the way of another vessel. The term 'vessel Restricted in her Ability to Manoeuvre' shall include but not be limited to:

(i)   A vessel engaged in laying, servicing, or picking up a Navigational mark, submarine cable or pipeline;

(ii)   A vessel engaged in dredging, surveying or Underwater operations;

(iii)   A vessel engaged in Replenishment or transferring persons, provisions or cargo while underway;

continued

(iv)   A vessel engaged in the launching or recovery of Aircraft;

(v)   A vessel engaged in Mine clearance operations;

(vi)   A vessel engaged in a Towing operation such as severely restricts the towing vessel and her tow in their ability to deviate from their course.

[**My mnemonic for this – and you will need to know these categories – is 'Never Use RAM** *thoughtlessly*'**]**

Shapes:

- Three shapes in a vertical line: a ball over a diamond over a ball.
- A rigid replica of International Code flag 'A' when engaged in diving operations and the vessel is too small to display the shapes fully.

Identification lights: Three all-round lights where best seen: red over white over red.

Side and sternlights: Sidelights and sternlights **only when making way through the water.**

Masthead lights:

- Standard masthead lights, but **only when making way through the water.**[8]
- When at anchor, but engaged in one of the activities that constitute RAM (*Rule 3(g)*), standard anchor lights plus RAM identification lights (except for vessels engaged in underwater operations, which don't show anchor lights).(*Rule 27(d)(iii)*.)

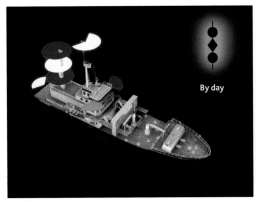

A vessel Restricted in its Ability to Manoeuvre, less than 50 metres in length, making way.

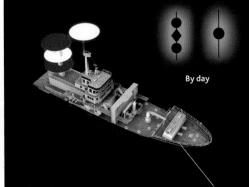

A vessel Restricted in its Ability to Manoeuvre, less than 50 metres in length, at anchor.

---

[8]There is one exception to this: Vessels engaged in mine clearance operations show masthead and side lights when under way, whether making way or not.

3

Notes:

■ As you can see from the definition, there is quite a mixed bag of activity that comes under the heading of RAM. It is, however, safe to say that all of these vessels will have difficulty taking unrestricted action to avoid a collision. Quite often too, for instance when ships are launching and recovering aircraft, they will be moving relatively fast.

■ Vessels which are RAM and NUC are considered the least manoeuvrable vessels, according to the Rules, so it is important that you know whether they are making way or not. Accordingly, with the exception of vessels engaged in mine clearance operations, they do not show side, stern or steaming lights when dead in the water.

■ Unlike vessels NUC, some of the RAM activities (for example, diving and underwater operations) can be conducted at anchor, so there is provision to show RAM lights and shapes from anchored vessels.

■ Towing vessels can legitimately hoist RAM shapes and lights alongside their other towing signals if the nature of the tow limits their ability to deviate from their course.

■ Vessels less than 12 metres in length need only show RAM shapes and lights when conducting diving operations.

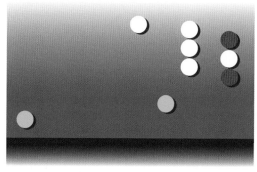

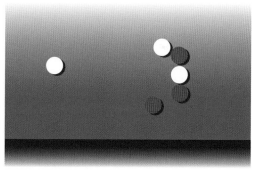

Tug and tow, longer than 200 metres in length, making way, severely restricted in their ability to deviate from their course. Seen from the starboard side.

Vessel Restricted in her Ability to Manoeuvre, making way, seen from her port side.

Dredgers and Vessels Engaged in Dredging or Underwater Operations (Rule 27)

Shapes:

- Three shapes in a vertical line: a ball over a diamond over a ball.
- Where an obstruction exists to one side or another: two balls in a vertical line on the side where an obstruction exists, and two diamonds on the side that other vessels may pass.
- When at anchor, vessels Restricted in their Ability to Manoeuvre conducting dredging or underwater operations, don't show anchor shapes. (*Rule 27(d)(iii)*.)

Identification lights:

- Three all-round lights where best seen: red over white over red.
- Where an obstruction exists to one side or another: two all-round red lights in a vertical line on the side where an obstruction exists, and two all-round green lights on the side that other vessels may pass.

Side and sternlights: Sidelights and sternlights **only when making way through the water.**

Masthead lights:

- Standard steaming lights, but **only when making way through the water**.
- When at anchor, vessels Restricted in their Ability to Manoeuvre conducting dredging or underwater operations, don't show anchor lights.(*Rule 27(d)(iii)*.)

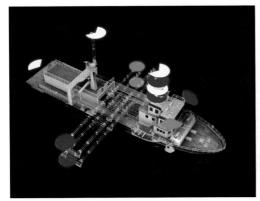

A vessel engaged in underwater operations that restricts her manoeuvrability, making way and obstructed on her starboard side.

A vessel engaged in diving operations that is too small to carry the lights and shapes. By day, she would fly Flag 'A'.

3

Notes:

■ 'Underwater Operations' can consist of diving, using remotely operated vehicles (little robotic diving machines for unmanned work under water), surveying or just about any other sub-surface business. To qualify for RAM, the operations must make manoeuvring difficult.

■ The lights are splendid: colours everywhere. But they can seem a little confusing – with side and steaming lights, RAM lights and obstruction lights. In practice, identification is generally easier on the water than it looks on paper. By day, you will certainly be able to identify a dredger by its appearance. They are universally ugly ships[9] that are quite often floodlit at night, and there is usually a continuous metallic clanking noise from their dredging gear when they are working. You do see a fair number of these around, and you should know how to recognise them.

■ A vessel engaged in diving operations that is too small to carry these lights and shapes need only carry a rigid version of Flag 'A' by day and three all-round lights: red-white-red, mounted vertically, by night.

The obstruction lights are quite easy to remember:

■ The obstruction lights are just like traffic lights: 'go' on green and 'stop' on red.

■ By day, you can pass the diamonds – 'diamonds are forever', but you will end up in trouble if you pass down the side with the balls (the 'balls-up' again, I'm afraid.)

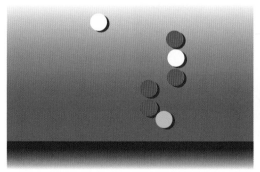

Vessel less than 50 metres in length, engaged in underwater operations. She is making way and obstructed on her starboard side.

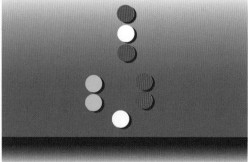

Vessel engaged in underwater or dredging operations, viewed from astern. She is making way and has an obstruction on her starboard side.

---

[9]Somewhere in the world, there is probably a beautiful dredger. If so, I would like to take this opportunity to apologise unreservedly for my remarks to the designer, skipper and crew of this remarkable – and certainly unique – vessel.

Mine Clearance Operations (Rule 27(f))

Shapes:

- Three balls: one at the masthead and one at each yardarm of the forward mast.
- No 'RAM' shapes are displayed.

Identification lights:

- Three all-round green lights: one at the masthead and one at each yardarm of the forward mast.
- No 'RAM' lights are displayed.

Side and sternlights: Standard for a power-driven vessel. **Shown when under way** (unlike all other vessels that are Restricted in their Ability to Manoeuvre that only show these lights when making way).

Masthead lights: Standard for a power-driven vessel. One or two, as appropriate, **shown when under way** (unlike all other vessels that are Restricted in their Ability to Manoeuvre which only show these lights when making way).

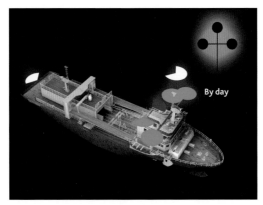

A vessel engaged in Mine Clearance operations, less than 50 metres in length, under way.

Notes:

- A very distinctive and unmistakable set of lights and shapes. There is, moreover, no shortage of explosive debris on or under the seabed that these ships quite regularly identify and destroy, some of it very unstable. Note the last sentence of Rule 27(f): 'These lights or shapes indicate that **it is dangerous for another vessel to approach within 1,000 metres** of the mine-clearance vessel.'That is half a mile to you and me: they mean it – don't go there.

- This is the only category of vessel Restricted in its Ability to Manoeuvre that shows side, stern and masthead lights when under way, but not making way. This is quite common: mine hunting is often conducted with the vessel 'hovering' in a stationary position over the seabed.

- Lights and shapes are also shown when the vessel is at anchor on mine-clearance operations. In this case, 'standard' anchor lights are also shown.

- Although these vessels don't carry 'RAM' shapes and lights, they are in every way Restricted in their Ability to Manoeuvre, and they may be operating divers or remote underwater devices.

There's a little American mnemonic for this: 'Three balls or three greens make mine hunting machines.'

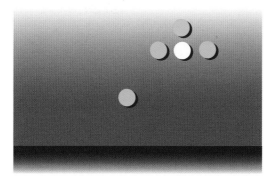

A vessel less than 50 metres long, engaged in mine clearance operations, under way and seen from her starboard side.

Vessel Constrained by her Draught (Rule 28)

Definition:

Rule 3(h)

- The term 'vessel Constrained by her Draught' means a power-driven vessel which, because of her draught in relation to the available depth of water and width of navigable water is severely restricted in her ability to deviate from the course she is following'.

Rule 28

- A vessel constrained by her draught may, in addition to the lights prescribed for power-driven vessels in Rule 23, exhibit where they can best be seen three all-round red lights in a vertical line, or a cylinder.

Shapes: A cylinder, where best seen.

Identification lights: Three red all-round lights, one above the other.

Side and sternlights: Sidelights and sternlights when under way, as for a power-driven vessel.

Masthead lights: As for a power-driven vessel when under way.

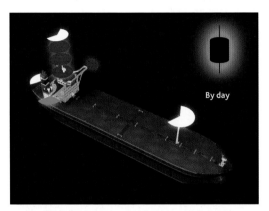

A vessel constrained by its draught, under way.

A vessel constrained by her draught (note the black cylinder circled in red) taken from a pretty exciting viewpoint.

3

Notes:

- You will note from Rule 28 that these lights and shapes are *not* mandatory, but if ships that are constrained by their draught choose not to display the lights and shapes, they can't really expect any priority. In practice, big ships will nearly always declare themselves to be constrained by their draught (when appropriate) in close-pilotage waters and make the appropriate signals. Sometimes the lights and shapes are altered by local by-laws: always read the Sailing Directions before approaching an unfamiliar port.

- Technically, these vessels are not 'Restricted in their Ability to Manoeuvre' because they are power-driven vessels constrained not by their employment, but by geography.

- They are, however, severely constrained in their ability to avoid a collision. It's a bit like the old joke: 'What do you call a 20-stone bouncer who is about to hit you? 'The answer is 'Anything he wants.' And that is how to treat a vessel constrained by its draught. It's heavy, it's committed to the channel and it can't easily stop. When it wants you to get out of the way . . . you really ought to do so!

- Only vessels Not Under Command and Restricted in their Ability to Manoeuvre are absolved from the need to avoid impeding a vessel constrained by its draught. (*Rule 18d.*)

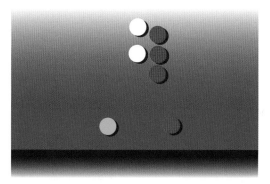

A vessel constrained by her draught, under way, from right ahead – just the place you don't want to be!

Vessels that cannot manoeuvre

Virtually all the vessels up to now have been under way – not attached to the shore or sea bed in any way. We will now have a look at vessels that simply cannot manoeuvre to keep clear of you: vessels that are **at anchor, or aground**. Straight away you will realise that the masthead lights, sidelights and sternlight, which are only shown by vessels under way, are redundant. The lights and shapes (and sound signals, come to that) have to be recognisably different from those of a vessel under way in order to make it easy for other mariners to realise that the burden of collision avoidance lies with them. The practical difficulty is in making the lights and shapes of an anchored vessel stand out – which they don't always manage. As always, if you are at all uncertain, the best advice is to proceed with caution, and if possible get another pair of eyes onto the problem.

Although the Rules are not specific about this, a vessel that is securely moored to a buoy may consider itself to be at anchor, but a vessel whose anchor is dragging should not. It is good practice to use your anchor light when moored to a buoy, especially in a large ship, mainly to avoid other people hitting you – but with the added advantage (for the yachtsmen among us) of helping you find your way back to the boat after an evening in the pub.

Vessels at Anchor (Rule 30)

Shapes:

- A ball in the fore part of the ship, where best seen.
- Vessels less than 7 metres in length, when anchored clear of narrow channels, fairways or anchorages, or normal navigation routes, need not exhibit a ball.

Identification lights:

- A white all-round light in the fore part of the ship, where best seen
- A second white all-round light in the stern of the vessel, but lower than that at the forward end.
- Vessels of less than 50 metres in length need show only one all-round light, where it can best be seen.
- Any vessel at anchor may show additional lights to illuminate her decks; a vessel of 100 metres in length, or more, must do this.
- Small boats of more than 7 metres must show an anchor light; vessels under 7 metres do not have to, provided they are clear of likely shipping routes.

A vessel less than 50 metres in length at anchor.

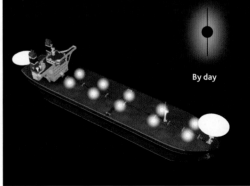

A vessel at anchor, possibly greater than 50 metres in length, showing two all-round white lights and deck working lights.

3

Notes:

- You will note that the height of the white all-round lights for vessels longer than 50 metres is the opposite of that for the masthead lights of power-driven vessels under way. Is there room for confusion?Not really; if they are the masthead lights, then where are the sidelights?And the big give-away is the deck working lights that are mandatory in big ships, and optional in smaller ones.
- The distinction between fore and aft is important, because it allows you to determine which end the cable is streamed from, and so give it a decent clearance.
- I have mentioned it before, but you will sometimes have to look quite hard to see the anchor ball on big ships, which is often displayed from a small stub mast right over the bows.

Vessels Aground (Rule 30)

Shapes:

- Three black balls in a vertical line
- Not necessary for vessels less than 12 metres in length. The embarrassed and rather sheepish look on the crew's faces will be enough!

Identification lights:

- Anchor lights appropriate to the length of the ship, the forward one being higher than the after one.
- Two all-round red lights in a vertical line, although this is not necessary for a vessel less than 12 metres in length that is aground.
- No need to illuminate the deck, irrespective of length.

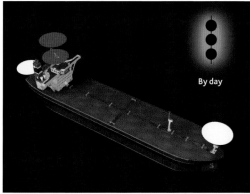

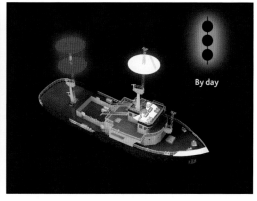

A vessel aground. Possibly greater than 50 metres in length.

A vessel aground, less than 50 metres in length.

Notes:

- There is no need for the deck working lights, because the red lights serve to distinguish this from a ship at anchor or a power-driven vessel under way.

- It cannot, of course, be confused with a vessel Not Under Command, because a vessel not under command shows side and sternlights if it is making way, or just the two red lights if it is stationary in the water.

- There is a bit of a trap for the unwary student of the Collision Regulations here. If you think about it there is a sort of logical progression:

    - At anchor – one ball – one white light
    - NUC – 2 balls – two red lights
    - Do not be seduced into thinking that a vessel aground therefore has three balls and three red lights – it doesn't: it has three balls and *two* red lights, together with anchor lights.

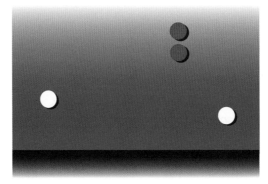

A vessel aground, possibly greater than 50 metres in length. Bow to the left.

Part 4: Some oddballs

I appreciate that that is already quite a lot to digest, but there are just a few categories of unusual vessels that you need to know about.

Hovercraft (Rule 23(b))

Shapes: None: the shape of a hovercraft – and the noise it makes – are unmistakable.

Identification lights: In the non-displacement mode, a yellow all-round light flashing at 120 flashes per minute, or more.

Side and sternlights: As for a power-driven vessel.

Masthead steaming lights: As for a power-driven vessel.

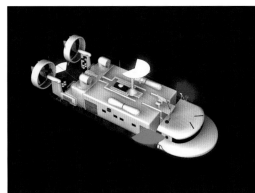
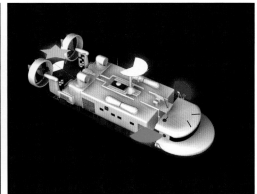

3

Hovercraft in the displacement mode – lit and behaves like a power driven vessel.

A hovercraft in the non-displacement mode. Lit and behaves like a power driven vessel, but with a flashing yellow light.

Notes:

- In the Rules, hovercraft are known as air-cushion vessels.

- They can operate in two modes: the displacement mode, when they are not hovering, but floating on the water. The alternative is in the non-displacement mode, when they are hovering. In either mode, they are lit and marked as standard power-driven vessels, and behave as such. However, when hovering (the 'non-displacement mode') they show a flashing yellow light. In the non-displacement mode they are a lot 'skiddier' in the turn than any 'normal' vessel, and a lot faster.

- There are not a lot of commercial hovercraft companies operating. One prominent route is across the Solent from Southsea to Ryde in the Isle of Wight.

- Bear in mind that they are very susceptible to a crosswind and often make good a course that is significantly different to their heading. At night, therefore, their navigation lights may be misleading.

- Don't confuse them with submarines just because they both show yellow or orange flashing lights. They look quite different, have different navigation light layouts and hovercraft travel much faster.

Seaplanes

Definitions:

Rule 3(e)

- The word 'seaplane' includes any aircraft designed to manoeuvre upon the water.

Rule 3(b)

- The term 'power driven vessel' means any vessel powered by machinery.

Notes:

- A seaplane carries no identifying lights or shapes. When under way on the water, they will normally carry a 'masthead light' in the front part of the fuselage and coloured navigation lights on the wingtips and a white sternlight at the back end.
- Seaplanes are required to keep clear of all other vessels and to avoid impeding their navigation (*Rule 18e*). If push comes to shove, however, they must be considered as power-driven vessels and manoeuvre accordingly. (*Rule 3b*.)

Wing-in-Ground Craft (Rule 23(c))

Definitions:

Rule 3(m)

- The word 'wing-in-ground (WIG) craft' means a multi-modal craft which, in its main operational mode, flies in close proximity to the surface by utilising surface-effect action.

Rule 23(c)

- A WIG craft only when taking off, landing and in flight near the surface shall, in addition to the lights prescribed in paragraph (a) of this Rule (those for power driven vessels under way), **exhibit a high-intensity all-round. flashing red light.**

Rule 31

- Where it is impractical for a seaplane or WIG craft to exhibit lights and shapes of the characteristics or in the positions prescribed in the Rules of this Part, she shall exhibit lights and shapes as closely similar in characteristics and position as is possible.

Notes:

- Like seaplanes, WIG craft should display (as closely as possible) lights for a power-driven vessel. In flight, however, it also carries a high intensity all-round flashing red light.
- These are quite remarkable craft that 'fly' at high speed just above the surface, using an aerodynamically induced air cushion to support themselves.
- We will come to it later, but Rule 18(f) instructs WIG craft to keep clear of other vessels when taking off, landing and in flight. When operating on the water, it should behave like a standard power-driven vessel.
- If you feel inclined, look up WIG craft on the Internet. It would scare the daylights out of me to have one of these extraordinary craft approaching me at 150 knots!

Vessels propelled by Oars (Rule 25(d)(ii))

Definitions:

3

Rule 25(d)(ii)

A vessel under oars may exhibit the lights prescribed in this Rule for sailing vessels, but if she does not, she shall have ready at hand an electric torch or lighted lantern showing a white light which shall be exhibited in sufficient time to prevent collision.

Notes:

- A vessel under oars could show sidelights and a sternlight, or a combined lantern, but is more likely to carry a white torch to let other vessels know it is there.

- A large Roman fighting galley with three banks of oars may choose to have something more assertive than a single white torch, but mercifully they are few and far between these days.

A vessel propelled by oars.

Police Boats

Police boats are reasonably common, particularly in busy and congested inshore waters. They are lit as power-driven vessels with a blue flashing light and, when necessary, a siren. Another clue comes from the big letters down the side which spell out **'P O L I C E'** or its local equivalent.

Lifeboats

British lifeboats carry a blue flashing light (1 flash per second) and standard navigation lights.

Warships and Submarines

Warships of just about all nations are painted a drab grey or off-grey colour and even at very great distances there is something about their centrally stacked superstructure that makes their profile stand out from merchant ships. Don't always expect them to behave or look like 'normal' ships. Their lights may also look a little unusual if the layout of the superstructure demands unconventional light placing. An aircraft carrier's lights, for instance, may be displaced off its centreline. You will often see warships with a set of red obstruction lights showing at the masthead to prevent helicopters flying into them at night, and you will occasionally see a warship with a helicopter on the flight deck that has a set of lights all of its own.

Submarines on the surface may have one or more of their lights very close to the surface, which can sometimes be obscured by the swell. They also use an orange or amber flashing light to identify themselves on the surface. Under water, they may release white or orange smoke candles which burn with a white flame at night. They may also release green or red flares from under water. The green flare is routine, but **the red flare is a distress signal**, and should be treated as such.

Oil and Gas Rigs

Oil and gas rigs tend to hang about in herds. You occasionally come across an isolated rig that has wandered off from its friends for a bit of peace and quiet, but more generally you find them peacefully grazing away together in the oil and gas fields. Permanent rigs are well charted, but I have often had difficulty keeping up with the exploratory rigs, which are sent out by the companies to find new deposits, and which are almost never shown on the charts – although their position is well documented in Notices to Mariners.

The rigs tend to be well lit. Many have a plume of flame burning off gasses into the atmosphere, and they often have safety boats hanging around nearby. Give them at least a ½-mile clearance, and don't forget to check the chart to make sure that there aren't any navigation warnings or restrictions in their vicinity.

Lights and Shapes – Size and Range (Rule 22, Annex I para 6)

The minimum visible ranges of lights are set out in Rule 22:

Vessels of 50 **metres or more in length**:

- Masthead light   6 miles
- Sidelight   3 miles
- Sternlight   3 miles
- Towing light   3 miles
- White, red, green or yellow all-round light   3 miles

continued

3

Vessels of 12 **metres or more, but less than 50 metres, in length**

- Masthead light   5 miles (3 if less than 20 metres in length)
- Sidelight   2 miles
- Sternlight   2 miles
- Towing light   2 miles
- White, red, green or yellow all-round light   2 miles

Vessels of less **than 12metres in length**:

- Masthead light   2 miles
- Sidelight   1 miles
- Sternlight   2 miles
- Towing light   2 miles
- White, red, green or yellow all-round light   2 miles

In **inconspicuous, partly submerged vessels or objects being towed**:

- White all-round light   3 miles

The minimum size of the proscribed shapes are set out in Annex I, para 6.

Black ball	Diameter not less than 0.6 metre
Cone	Diameter not less than 0.6 metre Height equal to diameter
Cylinder	Diameter not less than 0.6 metre Height twice the diameter
Diamond	Two cones, base together
- Vertical distance between shapes at least 1.5 metres. - Dimensions commensurately reduced for vessels smaller than 20 metres in length	

Signals to Attract Attention

3

Rule 36

If necessary to attract the attention of another vessel, any vessel may make light or sound signals that cannot be mistaken for any signal authorized elsewhere in these Rules, or may direct the beam of her searchlight in the direction of the danger, in such a way as not to embarrass any vessel. Any light to attract the attention of another vessel shall be such that it cannot be mistaken for any aid to navigation. For the purpose of this Rule the use of high intensity intermittent or revolving lights, such as strobe lights, shall be avoided.

The message contained in Rule 36 is unambiguous: if you need to attract attention, do so in a way that doesn't embarrass or mislead another vessel seeing the signal.

I have never been entirely convinced of the value of a searchlight playing on the water, or on a sail, to attract someone's attention: it is not always easy for another vessel to see or to interpret. Use it when you need to, but don't rely on it. You could also try:

■ Calling the other ship on VHF Channel 16[10], preferably by name. Don't however, put too much faith in the VHF for collision avoidance – you can't always guarantee getting through and even if you do, imperfect understanding may lead to more confusion, not less.

■ Sound signal: five or more short blasts.

■ If you are in a yacht and are worried about the possibility of being run down, you might want to turn away to reduce the closing rate and give yourself more time.

Do not:

■ Point a searchlight directly at the bridge of another ship.

■ Use a high-intensity strobe light.

■ Use distress flares. They carry one meaning, and one alone: that you need to be helped or rescued.

---

[10]See Chapter 12. The UK Coastguard has nominated the following channels as inter-ship working channels:

06, 08, 09, 10, 13, 15, 17, 67, 69, 72, 73, 77

Switch to one of these once you have made contact on Channel 16.

Of these, Channel 13 is designated for inter-ship safety of navigation ('bridge-to-bridge') and you may want to use this as a first reserve for Channel 16.

Chapter 3 – Self-test (Rules 20 – 31 and 36)

1. a. When *must* lights be shown and when *may* they be shown? (*Rule 20(b) and (c).*)

   b. When *must* shapes be exhibited?(*Rule 20(d).*)

2. a. What arcs does a masthead light show over? (*Rule 21(a).*)

   b. What arcs does a sternlight show over? (*Rule 21(c).*)

   c. What colour is a towing light? (*Rule 21(d).*)

3. What lights should a power-driven vessel of greater than 50 metres in length show at night, over what arcs?(*Rule 23(a).*)

4. What shape should a towing vessel and a vessel being towed show when the length of the tow is greater than 200 metres?(*Rule 24(a)(v), and (e)(iii).*)

5. What lights would each of these vessels show by night?(*Rule 24(a)(i) to (iv), (e)(i) and (e)(ii).*)

6. What shape does a sailing vessel display when it has its sails up and is motoring?(*Rule 25(e).*)

7. a. Do trawlers have to show masthead lights when under way?(*Rule 26(b).*)

   b. Do other fishing vessels?(*Rule 26(c).*)

8. What is the meaning of a single white all-round light in a vessel engaged in fishing, when shown in conjunction with fishing lights?(*Rule 26(c)(ii).*)

9. What shapes are shown by a vessel **not under command**?(*Rule 27(a)(ii).*)

10. What lights does a vessel engaged in mine clearance operations show?(*Rule 23 and 27(f).*)

11. What shape is shown by a Vessel Constrained by its draught?(*Rule 28.*)

12. What shapes would you expect to see on a vessel aground of more than 50 metres in length?(*Rule 30(d)(ii).*)

13. Fill in the blanks (Rule 36):

If necessary to attract the attention of another vessel, any vessel may make light or sound signals that cannot be mistaken for any signal authorized elsewhere in these Rules, or may direct the beam of her searchlight in the direction of the danger, in such a way as not to embarrass any vessel. Any light to attract the attention of another vessel shall be such that it cannot be mistaken for ____ ____ __ _____. For the purpose of this Rule the use of _____ _____ or _____ _____ such as strobe lights, shall be avoided.

4 Sound Signals: Rules 32–35

Read through Rules 32–35 before you start on this chapter.

There are two kinds of sound signal: **manoeuvring signals** and **fog signals**.

Manoeuvring signals are used by ships **in sight of each other** to help them understand each other's actions.

Fog signals are used in **restricted visibility** for two reasons:

- To let other vessels know that you are there
- To tell them, roughly speaking, what you are doing.

These are not mutually exclusive: in patchy (but nevertheless restricted) visibility, or on the edge of a fog bank, you may need to use both – but if you do, it is important to avoid any confusion.

Sound signals: (Rules 32, 33)

Prolonged blast: a blast of 4–6 seconds' duration

Short blast: a blast of about 1 second's duration.

Signalling devices to be carried by vessels:

- **A vessel more than 100 metres in length:** a bell and gong, or equipment that makes the same sound. And a whistle.
- **A vessel longer than 20 metres and less than 100:** a bell, or equipment that makes the same sound. And a whistle.
- **A vessel longer than 12 metres and less than 20:** a whistle.
- **A vessel less than 12 metres in length:** nothing prescribed, but she must have some means of making an efficient sound signal.

The frequencies and ranges of sound signalling equipment are set out in Annex III of the Rules.

Manoeuvring signals for vessels in sight of each other (Rule 34)

Manoeuvring signals are not difficult – which is handy, because they are very common, particularly in congested waterways or harbours and you need to know them. They are made by vessels that are in sight of each other in order to clarify the actions that they are taking.

According to the Rules, the 'turning or slowing down signals' in Rule 34(a) **are mandatory** for power-driven vessels, under way, that are in sight of each other and manoeuvring in accordance with the Rules.

Rule 34(a)

When vessels are in sight of one another, a **power-driven vessel under way,** when manoeuvring as authorized or required by these Rules, **shall** indicate that manoeuvre by the following signals on her whistle:

- one short blast to mean 'I am altering my course to starboard';
- two short blasts to mean 'I am altering my course to port';
- three short blasts to mean 'I am operating astern propulsion'.

These signals are only required of power-driven vessels, although the supplementary signals made by flashing light, can be made by any vessel. In practice, these supplementary light signals, made from an all-round white light at the masthead, are quite rare: I have only seen it once in 30-odd years at sea.

Rule 34(b)

Any vessel may supplement the whistle signals prescribed in paragraph (a) of this Rule by light signals, repeated as appropriate, whilst the manoeuvre is being carried out:

(i) These signals shall have the following significance:
  (i)   one flash to mean 'I am altering my course to starboard';
  (ii) two flashes to mean 'I am altering my course to port';
  (iii) three flashes to mean 'I am operating astern propulsion'.
(ii) The duration of each flash shall be about 1 second, the interval between flashes shall be about one second, and the interval between successive signals shall not be less than 10 seconds.
(iii) The light used for this signal shall, if fitted, be an all-round white light, visible at a minimum range of 5 miles, and shall comply with the provisions of Annex I to these Regulations.

4

Turning and Slowing Down Signals (Rule 34(a))

I am altering my course to starboard	One short blast	■
I am altering my course to port	Two short blasts	■ ■
I am operating astern propulsion	Three short blasts	■ ■ ■

Notes:

1. The third of these signals indicates 'I am operating astern propulsion', **not** 'I am going astern'. So you sound it as you put your engines astern, even if the ship is still moving ahead in the water.
2. These signals are only used by power-driven vessels, when they are in sight of another vessel.
3. A short blast is of about 1-second's duration.
4. Can be supplemented by an identical signal from the masthead with all-round white flashing light.

Manoeuvring Signals in a Narrow Channel or Fairway (Rule 34(c))

You can also use manoeuvring signals in a narrow channel or fairway to remove ambiguity when one vessel wishes to overtake another. This applies to any vessel, not just a power driven vessel, and allows the vessel being overtaken to signal her consent and move to the appropriate side of the fairway to make space for the passing vessel to come through.

Of course, in many such waterways you will carry a pilot and bridge-to-bridge communications will take place between pilots by VHF. But not always – and there is an enduring simplicity about these signals which makes them universally valuable.

Overtaking signals in a Narrow Channel or Fairway (Rule 34(c))

I intend to overtake you on your starboard side	Two prolonged blasts followed by one short blast	▬ ▬ ■
I intend to overtake you on your port side	Two prolonged blasts followed by two short blasts	▬ ▬ ■ ■
I am happy for you to overtake	One prolonged blast, one short blast, one prolonged blast, one short blast	▬ ■ ▬ ■
I am *not* happy for you to overtake	At least 5 short and rapid blasts	■ ■ ■ ■ ■

Continued

> **Notes:**
> 1. Once again, 'starboard' is indicated by a single short blast and 'port' by two short blasts. Only this time they have the prefix of two prolonged blasts (4–6 seconds) to indicate that this is an overtaking signal.
> 2. These signals may be used by *any* vessels in sight of each other, but only when proceeding along a narrow channel or fairway.
> 3. The hawk-eyed among you will instantly recognise that the fourth signal: 'I am *not* happy for you to overtake' is not stipulated in Rule 34(c). This is, however, very much in the spirit of Rule 34(d) and would be understood as such.

4

Rule 34(d). The signal of 'at least 5 short and rapid blasts' (Rule 34(d)) is the most common of all of these manoeuvring signals. The Rules politely suggest that it should be used 'when either vessel fails to understand the intention or actions of the other.' More often, in my experience, it is used to signal something along the lines of 'Get out of my way, you idiot!' It is a useful tool to have in your armoury.

Manoeuvring Signals when approaching a blind corner in a narrow channel (Rule 34(e))

This is the third and final manoeuvring signal for ships in sight of each other, available for any vessel to use as it approaches a blind corner in a narrow channel or fairway. It is frequently used.

Approaching a Blind Corner (Rule 34(e))

Approaching a bend or other area where approaching traffic might be obscured	1 prolonged blast	■■■■

Notes:
1. Vessels hearing this signal coming round a bend in the fairway should reply in kind: with a single prolonged blast (4–6 seconds).
2. If you do hear this signal coming from round the corner, take it seriously – it may well involve some fancy navigation. I once used it in the approach to a very tight, cliff-lined channel in the Norwegian Fjords. Sure enough, almost immediately there was an answering signal from around the corner. I squeezed as close to the starboard side of the channel as I could, in what was a pretty hopeless effort to make some space for the approaching vessel. It was only when I had all-but scraped the paint of the side of the ship that the pilot, with tears of mirth in his eyes, turned round and told me that 'There is often a very strong echo at this point of the Fjord. You should not think that there is another ship coming – *ja*?' I have always been suspicious of the Nordic sense of humour from that day to this.
3. The purist will question whether a sound signal from around a blind corner can properly constitute a signal between two ships in sight of each other. It is, however, an obvious extension of the clear visibility rules, and is not applied in restricted visibility.

Sound Signals in Restricted Visibility (Rule 35)

In this section, for the sake of simplicity, I have referred to 'Sound Signals in Restricted Visibility' as **'Fog Signals'**, even though there are a lot of other things that can reduce visibility (Rule 3(l)), including: mist, falling snow, heavy rainstorms, sandstorms or any other similar causes which might include smoke or dust storms.

Fog

However caused, you should be in no doubt that restricted visibility is the single, most dangerous situation that the majority of seafarers encounter – particularly in small vessels or yachts. My advice to anyone, particularly recreational sailors with less experience, is to watch the weather forecast like a hawk and do everything possible to avoid being out in poor visibility.

Fog changes everything: you have different manoeuvring rules, your level of uncertainty rises, navigation is more complex, other ships' movements are not obvious, and you have less time to avoid them. And on top of all that, your own periodic fog signals are loud, immediate, and consistently distracting. Vessels rely more on radar in restricted visibility, but small vessels often fail to show consistently on radar, or get lost in the ground clutter as the range closes, just at the point when they need to be at their most visible. Even if a ship posts additional lookouts, it always take time to report, and the speed of response will inevitably be slower. All-in-all, there are a lot of people doing their best in restricted visibility, but with imperfect data and moderately high levels of stress. Even to-day, with all of the technology at our disposal, this is not a good place to be.

A couple of things that you should have in the back of your mind in poor visibility are:

- **The other vessel may not have radar,** or it may be imperfectly tuned, or he may not be looking at it – so, no matter what size your ship is, or how diligently you make fog signals, there will be times when other vessels simply don't see you, or fail to properly assess your movements. It is unsafe to assume that other vessels will take appropriate action to avoid a collision. In restricted visibility, therefore, when vessels are not in sight of each other, all participants share responsibility for collision avoidance: there is no 'stand-on vessel'.

- **The Manoeuvring Rules change in, or close to, an area of restricted visibility when you can't see the other vessel.** The decision-making process is different and in many ways more complex.

- **Small vessels' radars are not good at bearings.** The way to decide whether risk of collision exists is through determining whether there is bearing movement, but the restricted size of a small boat's radar scanner, combined with the effect of more violent motion on a small flux-gate compass, means that the bearings will often be erratic and unreliable. So it takes longer for small boats to assess the risk, by which time the other vessel will be closer. If in doubt, small vessels should assume the worst and take early avoiding action, and large vessels should, where possible, give them space and a little tolerance.

- **AIS is useful.** I am a great believer that all competently operated vessels should carry not just an AIS receiver, but a transponder too, including recreational craft. It provides course, speed and identification data, and it removes a heap of uncertainty in fog.
- **A small vessel's foghorn may not be heard by big ships.** But there are plenty of smaller vessels out there who **will** hear it – so you must keep making the sound signals at the defined intervals in restricted visibility.
- **Don't always expect other ships to slow down in fog.** In inshore waters, ships may slow down to some extent, but in the shipping lanes, even in the Straits of Dover, you should expect some vessels still to be travelling quite fast. If you are going to belt through fog at high speed (and I would strongly discourage it), make sure that your radar is in tip-top condition, that it is properly and competently manned and that you have good lookouts, with reliable communications, wherever necessary. The issues surrounding **'safe speed'** are set out in Rule 6(a) and (b). We will come back to them in a later chapter, but bear in mind the two critical decisions that you need to make (Rule 6):
  a. Am I confident that I am able to **take proper and effective action to avoid a collision**?
  b. Am I able to **stop within a distance appropriate to the prevailing circumstances and conditions**?

Fog Signals

In restricted visibility, all vessels are assumed to be equally responsible for collision avoidance – no one can rely on the fact that they will be detected and given priority by other vessels. So the purpose of fog signals is quite simply to inform – to tell other vessels that you are there, and to give some indication of what you are doing.

Vessels Under Way

Power-driven Vessels (Rule 35(a) and (b))

Power-driven vessel under way and making way	One prolonged blast	Interval of not more than 2 minutes	
Power-driven vessel under way, but not making way. (ie, stopped in the water)	Two prolonged blasts with intervals of 2 seconds between blasts	Interval of not more than 2 minutes	

Notes:

1. These are by far the most common sound signals in restricted visibility.
2. If you are making the signals by hand, set a timer of some sort to make sure that you get the timing right: it is easy to forget when a number of other things are going on around you.

The Rogues' Gallery (Rule 35(c), (d) and (e))

Vessel *Not* under command	One prolonged blast followed by 2 short blasts	Interval of not more than 2 minutes	▬ ■ ■
Vessel <u>R</u>estricted in its ability to manoeuvre			
Vessel <u>C</u>onstrained by its draught			
<u>S</u>ailing vessel			
Vessel <u>E</u>ngaged in fishing			
Vessel engaged in <u>T</u>owing or pushing another vessel			

Notes:

1. If a vessel is making this signal, she does not make the signal of a power-driven vessel.
2. In a small sailing vessel, I would normally start the engine when fog comes in to improve my ability to manoeuvre. That done, I would make the sound signals for a power-driven vessel making way, rather than those for a sailing vessel.
3. The interesting thing is that restricted visibility, in the eyes of the rule-makers, puts fishing vessels and vessels not under command on the same scale of vulnerability. This underlines the fact that no one, not even the most severely restricted vessels, can assume that they will be given priority in poor visibility.
4. My mnemonic for these categories is: '<u>N</u>o <u>R</u>adar <u>C</u>an <u>S</u>ee <u>E</u>very <u>T</u>arget'.

And one exception . . .

Vessel being towed, or the last vessel in a tow (if manned)	One prolonged blast followed by 3 short blasts	Interval of not more than 2 minutes	▬ ■ ■ ■

Notes:

1. This is an important one: if you encounter a tow, you need to know where the back end is.
2. In order to avoid confusing other ships, this sound is made immediately after the towing vessel's signal.
3. If you want to maintain your unblemished no-claims bonus, try to make sure that the two signals, that of the tow, and that of the towing vessel, are both drawing past you in the same direction.

In practice, about 95 per cent of all shipping are power-driven vessels making way, sounding '—' every two minutes), and most of the remainder will sit firmly in the 'Rogues' Gallery', making '— ● ●' every two minutes. There are, however, a few more fog signals that you must know.

Vessels at Anchor and Aground

4

A vessel at anchor in fog is just about as dangerous as an uncharted rock suddenly appearing in the middle of a previously navigable channel. If you hear the bells and gongs, and you have a good idea what the source of the sound is, bear in mind that the length of the ship and her anchor cable may extend some distance from the source of the sound.

The routine sound signals proscribed for an anchored vessel are quite distinctive, but they are also of a very much shorter range than those for a vessel under way. (Which is why the time interval between signals is correspondingly shorter.)

It is also why a louder signal made by whistle '● — ●'[1] has been included for the use of anchored ships that are worried about the intentions of another vessel in their vicinity. This is both reassuring and practical if you have anchored in a busy stretch of water.

Vessels at anchor (Rule 35(g))		
Vessel of less than 100 metres in length	5 seconds ringing of a bell	Intervals of not more than 1 minute
Vessel of more than 100 metres in length	5 seconds ringing of a bell forward Followed immediately by: 5 seconds sounding of a gong aft	
Vessel at anchor giving warning of her position and indicating the possibility of a collision with an approaching vessel	As above But in addition: One short, one prolonged and one short blast on the whistle	

Notes:

1. Always give an anchored vessel a good berth in restricted visibility; not only can you not see his anchor cable, but you will be influenced by the tidal steam and he won't.
2. Don't rely on hearing this signal until you are very close: check out contacts that appear to be stationary on radar or AIS carefully to give yourself some advanced warning.
3. When you are at anchor in reduced visibility, it is quite reassuring to have the whistle signal of a short, a long and a short blast to warn people of your presence. Don't hesitate to use it if you are worried.

---

[1] Sad, but true: my mnemonic for this is that it looks a bit like a vessel, seen from astern, with large inflatable fenders down each side – worried that someone may hit her.

4

Vessels aground (Rule 35(h))

Vessel of less than 100 metres in length	3 distinct rings on a bell	Intervals of not more than 1 minute
	5 seconds ringing of a bell	
	3 distinct rings on a bell	
Vessel of more than 100 metres in length	3 distinct rings on a bell	
	5 seconds ringing of a bell forward	
	3 distinct rings on a bell	
	Followed immediately by:	
	5 seconds sounding of a gong aft	
Vessel aground giving warning of her position and indicating the possibility of a collision with an approaching vessel	As above	
	But in addition:	
	One short, one prolonged and one short blast on the whistle	

Notes:

1. This is quite simple: it extends the 5-seconds bell-ringing of a vessel at anchor with 3 'separate and distinct' rings on a bell before and after.
2. There is no reason why you should not make the whistle signal ('● — ●') as well if you choose to do so. It may help someone else avoid the mudbank.

And Finally . . .

Pilot vessels. They make the **appropriate fog signal** for a power-driven vessel, depending on whether they are under way, making way or at anchor. (We will draw a veil over the possibility of a pilot vessel running aground in fog.) This is **followed by four short blasts** to identify her as a pilot vessel.

Smaller vessels. Rules for sound signals in smaller vessels changed subtly in the 2003 amendment to the Rules (Rule 33): a **vessel greater than 12 metres** should carry a whistle. A **vessel longer than 20 metres and less than 100 metres** should carry a bell as well as a whistle. **Vessels longer than 100 metres** should carry a whistle, bell and gong. As a result:

■ A vessel of less than 12 metres in length is not obliged to give the proscribed signals, but must make some other efficient signal at intervals of not more than 2 minutes. Most of us use an aerosol fog-horn, and I would also carry one in a dinghy or tender in bad visibility. (*Rule 35(j)*.)

■ A vessel of more than 12 metres but less than 20 metres, when aground or at anchor, need not give the bell signals, but must make some other efficient signal at intervals of not more than 2 minutes. (*Rule 35(i)*.)

4

What can a yachtsman do with his limited resources in fog?

1. Make yourself as visible as possible with a good radar reflector and navigation lights.
2. Brief your crew to put down their novels and to keep a good and reliable lookout – and to listen out too.
3. Slow down to a safe speed (Rule 19), particularly if you are in a motor boat.
4. If you are sailing start your engine – or at least test it and have it ready for immediate use.
5. If you carry radar, have your most experienced crew manning it constantly for collision avoidance.
6. Put on lifejackets and have a grab-bag handy. This isn't melodramatic; it is sensible, good seamanship.
7. Have good intelligence: know what direction the predominant traffic is likely to approach you from and if possible keep clear of the busiest lanes.
8. If you find yourself in a steamy situation, turn to parallel the traffic flow until it calms down again.
9. Finally, know your fog signals. It will help you make informed decisions.

Sounds made by navigation marks. They make a variety of sound signals, which are always annotated on the chart.

■ **Explosive.** Detonation of an explosive device That sounds like a gun.
■ **Diaphone (dia).** This device, powered by compressed air, creates a low droning, hooting noise, actually on two frequencies simultaneously. It sounds deeply depressing and sometimes ends in a 'grunt'! If you have never heard one, you can while away many a happy hour in their company by searching for 'diaphone' on one of the Internet video sites.
■ **Foghorn (horn).** Uses compressed air or electricity to operate a diaphragm.
■ **Reed.** Also operated by compressed air, but is generally higher in pitch than a diaphone or horn.
■ **From buoys**, you are likely to hear **bells, whistles or gongs**. These may be mechanical, or just operating with the movement of the swell, in which case the sound will clearly be irregular. They will have a much shorter range than a ship's whistle, or shore-based sound signals. All will be marked on the chart, and they will be designed to make sure that they are positively different from any sound signal that a vessel might make.

Chapter 4 – Self-test (Rules 32–35)

1. a. What is the duration of a 'short blast'? (*Rule 32(b)*.)
   b. What is the duration of a 'prolonged blast'? (*Rule 32(c)*.)

   a. What is the manoeuvring signal for: 'I am altering my course to starboard? (*Rule 34(a)*.)
   b. What kind of vessel is required to make it? (*Rule 34(a)*.)
   c. Under what conditions of visibility is it made? (*Rule 34(a)*.)

2. a. How would you tell another vessel, which you can see, that you are about to overtake her on her starboard side in a narrow channel? (*Rule 34(c)(i)*.)
   b. What sound signal would he make if she was content? (*Rule 34(c)(ii)*.)

3. Complete the first line of Rule 35:
   ____ or ____ an area of restricted visibility, whether by ___ or ____, the signals proscribed in this Rule shall be used as follows . . .

4. a. What are the six categories of vessel that make the signal '— ● ●' in restricted visibility?
   b. How often should these vessels sound it? (*Rule 35(c)*.)

5. What signal should a vessel Restricted in its Ability to Manoeuvre make, when carrying out her work at anchor? (*Rule 35(d)*.)

6. a. What sound signal should a vessel of 127 metres in length make at anchor?
   b. How would that differ from a vessel of 87 metres in length?
   c. How often should they make these signals? (*Rule 35(g)*.)

7. If you go aground in a vessel of 149 metres in thick fog, what sound signal should you make (other than heart-felt groaning from the chart house)? (*Rule 35(h)*.)

8. Complete Rule 3(l):
   The term 'Restricted Visibility' means any condition in which visibility is restricted by ___, ____, ____ ____, ____ ____, ____ or any other similar causes.

9. What sound signal does a pilot vessel on pilotage duty make? (*Rule 35(k)*.)

5 The Manoeuvring Rules: *Rules 8, 11–19*

Read through Rules 8, 11–19 before you start on this chapter.

If you have understood the previous two chapters – how to recognise other vessels at sea – you are well on the way towards developing a good understanding of the Collision Regulations[1].

The Manoeuvring Rules establish the way in which vessels are expected to behave towards each other at sea. You will notice that the Rules don't specifically refer to a vessel having 'right of way.' They refer instead to a 'stand-on' vessel (green in the subsequent diagrams) and the 'give-way vessel' (shown in red). The reason for this is that the Manoeuvring Rules depend on co-operative behaviour to keep vessels safe, particularly at close quarters, and ultimately collision avoidance is everyone's responsibility. Even as the 'stand-on vessel', you must always be confident that sufficient action is being taken by the other vessel to avoid a collision. If you aren't happy, you are expected to do something about it.

It is, however, immensely useful if the stand-on vessel maintains some consistency in course and speed (*Rule 17(a)(i)*). Large ships tend to take avoiding action at a range of 5–3 miles, depending on the circumstances. If, however, at a slightly longer range (say 5–10 miles) you believe that a close quarters situation might develop, there is nothing to prevent either vessel from making an alteration of course or speed that would avoid the problem altogether.

Three Guiding Principles

In my own mind, I have found it easier to understand the Manoeuvring Rules by distilling the logic down into three 'Guiding Principles', which summarise the way in which vessels should behave towards each other on the high seas. These Principles have no authority within the Rules: they are my own interpretation, and I have set them out here solely because they are a useful framework for better understanding the Rules. They are:

1. **At sea, you drive on the right – and that broadly dictates the actions that you take for collision avoidance.**
2. **In general, more manoeuvrable vessels are required to give way to those that are less manoeuvrable.**
3. **In restricted visibility, when not in sight of each other, all vessels are equally responsible for taking action to avoid a collision.**

---

[1] I have always found it rather quaint that the principal authority for staying safe at sea is called 'The Collision Regulations'. It's a bit like saying that you are taking a crash course in driving.

Driving on the Right. The 'convention' of the Rules is that **at sea, you drive on the right**. Think about this in the context of motoring in a country that drives on the right: on the highway you will always pass oncoming traffic left-hand side to left-hand side: to try to do anything else would be suicidal. In fact, in almost any close encounter with another vehicle your first instinct will be to turn to the right to avoid a collision. **And so it is at sea: the Rules and the system of prioritisation have been created in such a way that turning to starboard will,** *in general,* **be preferable to turning to port as a means of avoiding a collision.**

This is not always the case, and every situation needs to be judged on its merits. However if you find yourself wanting to alter course to port to avoid a close-quarters situation, just give it a few seconds' extra thought before putting the rudder over. In particular, ask yourself the question: 'If I turn to port, what will happen if the other guy follows "the convention" and alters to starboard?'

The Swarm Instinct. Don't be alarmed when the whole horizon seems to be full of ships – all aiming at you. I have been watch-keeping at sea in one form or another for most of my life, and this seems to happen quite regularly. I have concluded that I must possess some hormone, still unknown to medical science, which makes me completely irresistible to large steel ships. The trick is to consider them one at a time, starting from the most dangerous.

A few tips:

- Closer vessels are generally a more immediate problem than those that are further away. Start with the closest and work your way out.

- Some will be closing you faster than others. Don't waste too much time on those that are closing very slowly, or opening.

- If you find that you are getting overloaded, and this happens to us all from time to time, get crew members to watch individual ships. As a first iteration, if the vessels are moving against the background (cloud, land or distant ships), they are probably not going to hit you because they are probably not on a steady bearing (see Chapter 2).

- Keep a good lookout and identify problems early. In particular, *always* look over your shoulder before altering course.

THE MANOEUVRING RULES

The rules change if you cannot see the other vessel because of restricted visibility. I have therefore divided this section into two parts:

1 **Rules that apply when vessels are in sight of each other, and**

2 **Rules that apply in restricted visibility.**

In terms of any single interaction, these are pretty much mutually exclusive: either you can see the other vessel or you cannot. But when you have a number of contacts around you, and you are manoeuvring in the vicinity of a fog bank or in patchy visibility, it is entirely possible that some vessels will be visible and others won't. In which case, you will have to apply both sets of rules at the same time.

The rules for narrow channels or fairways, and for Separation Schemes apply in all conditions of visibility, and I will deal with them separately in Chapter 6.

Rules that apply when vessels are in sight of each other: In reality, the great majority of interactions are between vessels of broadly similar manoeuvrability – two power-driven vessels, for instance, or two vessels under sail. However, the Rules do also define a 'hierarchy' of precedence (*Rule 18*) between vessels of unequal manoeuvrability in sight of each other. This hierarchy is designed to ensure that more manoeuvrable vessels keep out of the way of those that are less manoeuvrable.

Rules that apply in restricted visibility: In restricted visibility, it is very much more difficult. You can never be quite certain what the other vessel is doing, and how much knowledge of your movements he has. Some contacts may just never show up on your radar, and in any case your reaction times will undoubtedly be slower. As a result, the rules for manoeuvring in restricted visibility are more subtle, designed to remove all probability of a collision by sharing responsibility equally between vessels.

Sound signals in restricted visibility are not easy to correlate to radar contacts, but they do alert you when a contact is relatively close, and they may also help you to differentiate between power-driven vessels and those which are less manoeuvrable. They are absolutely necessary, but like so many aspects of restricted visibility, they provide no more than one part of the picture.

Part 1: Rules for vessels in sight of each other

Bear in mind the **mandatory** requirement (Rule 34(a) and (b)) for power-driven vessels to make sound signals, by day or night, when they are in sight of each other and manoeuvring in accordance with the Rules. This may not always happen in practice, but you should always make these signals when it serves to remove ambiguity – and it is certainly part of the expected response in a Rule of the Road exam.

Two unencumbered power-driven vessels

This is by far the most common form of encounter at sea. Vessels meet from three different aspects, each of which demands its own avoiding manoeuvres. They are:

- Head-on
- Crossing
- Overtaking

Head-on (Rule 14)

This is the first and most simple of the interactions: when two vessels are approaching each other 'ahead or nearly ahead.' Ships drive on the right at sea, so each of them should alter course to starboard, making one short blast as they go.

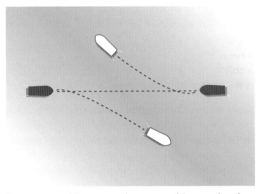

Two power-driven vessels approaching each other, head-on.

There is no clear dividing line between a head-on situation and a crossing situation, where two ships are closing each other from a broader angle. This is deliberate: as long as one or both of the vessels alter course to starboard (the convention), sounding one short blast, there is not going to be a problem. If one of them tries to alter to port, however, and the other to starboard, it could result in an expensive repair bill.

This is so simple that you would expect there to be a catch. And there is, albeit a very minor one. What do you do if the other vessel, closing from ahead on a reciprocal course, looks likely to pass close to starboard? In this instance, altering to starboard will, initially at least, *reduce* your passing distance. The trouble is that an alteration to port is potentially more risky because it could put you directly in her path if she alters to starboard.

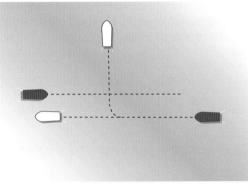

Do you alter to starboard . . .   . . . or just stand on?

This happened to me once on a fog-bound passage south across the Bay of Biscay, when I encountered a fishing vessel approaching from the south. In the end, because she wasn't altering and I didn't want to cross her bows, she emerged from the fog at about 500 metres and we passed within about 100 metres of each other, leaving me pretty rattled on the bridge. I am not certain that the fishing boat even knew we were approaching: when I passed her (it was about 1100 in the morning) I could hear loud music coming from the bridge and a cheerful figure in his underwear shuffled out onto the bridge wing to give me a sleepy wave.

There is no set answer to this, but if it happens to you (and it will), you should take early action to resolve it if possible: hold your nerve and stand on, or turn to starboard and cross her bows at a good, safe distance.

Crossing Situation (Rule 15)

When two power-driven vessels are crossing on a steady bearing, a collision will only be avoided if one of them alters either course or speed. It is both courteous and sensible that this alteration should result in the give-way vessel passing astern of the other vessel if at all possible. Since we have already established that turning to starboard is the expected and conventional way of avoiding a collision, it follows that the give-way vessel should be that one which, by turning to starboard, will pass astern of the other vessel.

5

If you work that out on a piece of paper, it works rather like traffic lights:

- If you can see the other vessel's green navigation light (if you are approaching from her starboard side) – you stand on.
- If you can see her red navigation light (you are approaching from her port side) – you must give way.

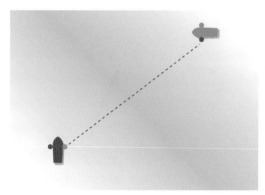
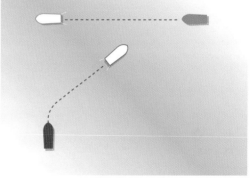

The green vessel can see the other's green navigation light . . . . . . so he stands on.

One short blast and alter course to starboard.

The red vessel can see the other's red navigation light . . . . . . so he must give way.

As the give-way vessel, don't try to pass ahead of the other vessel unless you can give her enough space to avoid causing her anxiety. If you don't have the sea room to make this work – or if other traffic makes a turn to the right impossible – you may have to slow down or stop. Meanwhile, the stand-on vessel should maintain its course and speed: we will look at how long she must hold her nerve for at the end of this section.

Alterations of course should always stand out to the other vessel, but they need not be too rigid. For instance, if the give-way vessel wants to press on and not lose too much time, a smart way of manoeuvring would be to alter to starboard and point a certain distance astern of the stand-on

5

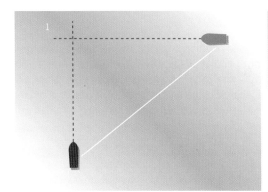

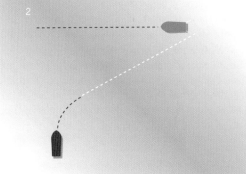

Steady bearing.

Red vessel makes 1 short blast and alters course to pass astern of the green vessel.

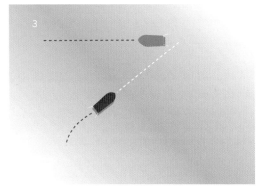

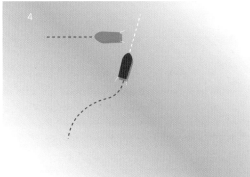

vessel – a distance that both ships will feel comfortable with. As the crossing vessel tracks through, you gently alter your course to follow the same aiming point astern of the other vessel until you get back to your original course.

Overtaking Situation (Rule 13)

This is one area where the convention of always altering to starboard does not necessarily apply. An overtaking vessel can alter either way, depending on the circumstances.

You are assumed to be overtaking another vessel if you are approaching it from within the arc of the other vessel's sternlight. In other words, when you are approaching it from more than 22.5 degrees abaft either beam. If you are in any doubt about this, and in daylight it is not always easy to tell, you should assume that you are the overtaking vessel and behave accordingly.

The logic here is quite reasonable: no one is forcing you to overtake the other vessel, so if you do so, you overtake at your own risk. Therefore:

> As an overtaking vessel, you must remain clear of the other vessel until you are finally past and clear, irrespective of the nature of the two vessels concerned.

This applies in all cases where the two vessels can see each other, including narrow channels and Separation Schemes. Even if the vessel being overtaken alters course halfway through the overtaking manoeuvre to create a crossing situation, the responsibility for collision avoidance still remains with the formerly overtaking vessel. It also applies to every category of ship, irrespective of its manoeuvrability: a vessel restricted in its ability to manoeuvre, for instance, overtaking a normal power-driven vessel is obliged to remain out of the way of the vessel being overtaken until she is 'finally past and clear'.

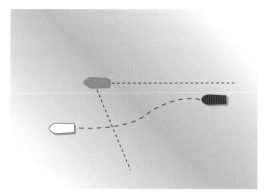

The red vessel is approaching from more than 22½ degrees abaft the green vessel's beam, and the two vessels can see each other . . .   . . . so red is the 'overtaking vessel'.

Alter to one side, making the appropriate sound signal and remain clear until finally past and clear.

5

It does not apply, however, in restricted visibility when the vessels cannot see each other for the simple reason that the relative geometry of the two ships is unclear.

Sailing Vessels (Rule 12)

The Rules for collision avoidance between sailing vessels under sail refer, naturally enough, to the direction of the wind. Many yachtsmen would speak about 'the vessel on the port tack', while the Rules refer to 'the vessel with the wind on the port side'. Don't allow this to confuse you: they both mean precisely the same thing.

> **Tack**: in square-rigged sailing vessels, the 'tack' was the rope used to carry the weight of wind in the sail. It was attached to the bottom windward corner of the courses (the lower square sails) and made fast to the ship's side. Thus, with the wind blowing from the starboard side, the weight would be carried 'on the starboard tack'. This incidentally led to the subsequent use today of the word 'tack' for the lower windward corner of the fore-and-aft sails that we use to-day.

> In the context of the Rules, if a sailing vessel is carrying its mainsail (or its largest for-and-aft sail) on its starboard side, the wind is deemed to be blowing from the vessel's port side and it is therefore on the port tack – and vice versa.

Mercifully **there are only three rules** for general collision avoidance between sailing vessels (as opposed to numerous racing rules that we need not bother with here):

First Rule: When two sailing vessels are approaching each other on different tacks, the vessel on the port tack gives way to the vessel on the starboard tack[2].

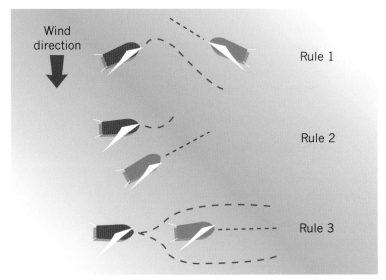

Sailing boats approaching each other from different angles. The three rules illustrated.

Second Rule: When two sailing vessels are closing each other on the same tack, the vessel to leeward has right of way.

Third Rule: The overtaking rule applies to sailing boats too. If one sailing boat is approaching another from more than 22.5 degrees abaft the beam, it becomes the overtaking vessel, irrespective of the wind direction or tack. It therefore has to remain clear.

Responsibilities between different types of vessel – 'the hierarchy' (Rule 18)

Although the great majority of interactions occur between two fully-manoeuvrable power-driven vessels, the Rules also make provision for encounters between two vessels that are not equally manoeuvrable. On these occasions, the more manoeuvrable vessel is required to give way to the other in accordance with the 'hierarchy' established in Rule 18.

---

[2]My way of remembering this is that the word 'starboard' is bigger than the word 'port'. Might is right – so starboard gets to stand on.

This pecking order is solely determined by a vessel's manoeuvrability. Look at the wording of Rule 18: it does not talk of rights of way, stand-on or give-way vessels. The term that this rule uses is: '. . . *shall keep out of the way of* . . .' and occasionally: '. . . *shall not impede* . . .'.

There is no specific distinction made between vessels Restricted in their Ability to Manoeuvre and those Not Under Command. The behaviour of these vessels depends very much upon their specific circumstances.

Seaplanes on the water and WIG craft in flight are required to keep 'well clear of all other vessels and avoid impeding their navigation'.[3] On the other hand, WIG craft on the water, hovercraft and hydrofoils are all classed as power-driven vessels, and are expected to manoeuvre accordingly.

And finally, a power-driven vessel stopped in the water still has responsibilities under this rule: it is under way and so must play its part in collision avoidance.

You will see that there are three exceptions to this eminently sensible rule:

- Overtaking (*Rule 13*)
- Narrow channels and fairways (*Rule 9*)
- Separation schemes (*Rule 10*)

The overtaking rule applies at all times when the two vessels are in sight of each other. If a vessel that is Restricted in its Ability to Manoeuvre decides to overtake a sailing vessel, for instance, Rule 13 would demand that he remains clear of the sailing vessel 'until finally past and clear'. We will deal with the particular issues of narrow channels and fairways, and Separation Schemes in Chapter 6.

Rule 18

Except where Rule 9, 10, and 13 otherwise require:

(a) A power-driven vessel under way shall keep out of the way of:

   (i)   A vessel Not Under Command;

   (ii) A vessel Restricted in her Ability to Manoeuvre;

   (iii) A vessel Engaged in Fishing;

   (iv) A sailing vessel;

continued

---

[3]Seaplanes must comply with the Rules, as if a power-driven vessel, where risk of collision exists.

(b)   A sailing vessel under way shall keep out of the way of:

    (i)   A vessel Not Under Command;

    (ii)   A vessel Restricted in her Ability to Manoeuvre;

    (iii) A vessel Engaged in Fishing;

(c)   A vessel Engaged in Fishing when under way shall, so far as possible, keep out of the way of:

    (i)   A vessel Not Under Command;

    (ii)   A vessel Restricted in her Ability to Manoeuvre;

(d)

    (i)   Any vessel other than a vessel Not Under Command or a vessel Restricted in her Ability to Manoeuvre shall, if the circumstances of the case admit, avoid impeding the safe passage of a vessel Constrained by her Draught, exhibiting the signals in Rule 28.

    (ii)   A vessel Constrained by her Draught shall navigate with particular caution having full regard to her special condition.

(e)   A seaplane on the water shall, in general, keep well clear of all vessels and avoid impeding their navigation. In circumstances, however, where risk of collision exists, she shall comply with the Rules of this Part.

(f)

    (i)   A WIG craft shall, when taking off, landing and in flight near the surface, keep well clear of all other vessels and avoid impeding their navigation.

    (ii)   A WIG craft operating on the water surface shall comply with the Rules of this Part as a power-driven vessel.

'Power gives way to sail'

Both as a ship-driver and a yachtsman, I have on a number of occasions heard people invoke Rule 18 in the familiar old adage that 'power gives way to sail' – evidently expecting larger merchant ships to keep clear of small recreational sailing boats. This is dangerous.

In general, I would expect small power boats to give way to sailing vessels. Large power-driven vessels, however, are different. If you think about it, yachtsmen drive just about the most manoeuvrable vessels on the water, and intelligent early action by a sailing boat, or a motor boat for that matter, will often prevent a close-quarters situation from occurring. It is therefore often unnecessary for a sailing vessel to plough on across the bows of a large merchant ship expecting it to alter course – and a little foolhardy too. For a start, you may not even have been seen from the ship's bridge. And even if she has seen you, the ship may not be able to change course and speed in time to avoid a fast-moving close contact. But the point is that, with a little intelligence the yacht should not be in that position anyway. Safety on the water requires co-operation and understanding from all mariners.

In the final analysis, however, the Rules are quite specific and – outside narrow channels, Separation Schemes and overtaking (and not counting vessels NUC, RAM and Constrained by their Draught) – a power-driven vessel that runs down a sailing vessel will be held liable under the Rules.

Action by the Give-way and Stand-on Vessels (Rules 16 and 17)

5

The Give-way Vessel (Rule 16)

If you have to give way, make your alteration of course and speed unambiguous to the stand-on vessel. This is your opportunity for the grand operatic gesture – don't nibble at it or leave it to the last minute! You only have to be on the receiving end of 'nibbling' a few times – wondering whether the give-way vessel is going to give you enough space – to persuade you that the 'early and substantial action' called for in Rule 16 is both appropriate and necessary.

Every situation is different, and the Rules are rightly not overly prescriptive about what action you should and should not take as the give-way vessel, other than the need for 'early and substantive action to keep well clear'. However, try to avoid passing close ahead of the other vessel, or turning to port when there is a possibility that she could turn to starboard and make the situation worse, or indeed doing anything that another vessel would find confusing or puzzling.

For good measure, to help the other guy understand your intentions, power-driven vessels are also obliged to make the manoeuvring sound signals (*Rule 34(a)*, supplemented as necessary by light signals (*Rule 34(b)* when altering course in accordance with the Rules.

It is worth reading Rule 16 in conjunction with Rule 8 (a) to (d):

Rule 16

Every vessel which is directed to keep out of the way of another vessel shall, so far as possible, take early and substantial action to keep well clear.

Rule 8 (partial)

(a) Any action to avoid collision shall be taken in accordance with the Rules of this Part and shall, if the circumstances of the case admit, be positive, made in ample time and with due regard to the observance of good seamanship.

(b) Any alteration of course and/or speed to avoid collision shall, if the circumstances of the case admit be large enough to be readily apparent to another vessel observing visually or by radar; a succession of small alterations of course and/or speed shall be avoided.

(c) If there is sufficient sea room, alteration of course alone may be the most effective action to avoid a close-quarters situation provided that it is made in good time, is substantial and does not result in another close-quarters situation.

(d) Action taken to avoid collision with another vessel shall be such as to result in passing at a safe distance. The effectiveness of the action shall be carefully checked until the other vessel is finally past and clear.

Rule 16 applies when vessels can see each other, and Rule 8 in any visibility – but the underlying message is the same: don't mess around. An alteration of course will generally be more easily discernable than changing your speed, but either action is available to you.

Finally, don't forget to always check how effective your manoeuvre has been. If you haven't succeeded in driving bearing movement by your chosen manoeuvre, try again.

The Stand-on Vessel (Rule 17)

There are three stages of discomfort for stand-on vessels:

- **Stage 1.** Initially, the stand-on vessel should maintain her course and speed (keeping a consistently wary eye on the give-way vessel).

- **Stage 2**. Then, 'as soon as it becomes apparent that the vessel required to keep out of the way is not taking appropriate action', the stand-on vessel *may* take necessary action to manoeuvre in such a way as to avoid a collision. In this case, try not to make this alteration of course to port if the other vessel is on your port side: if you do, you can almost guarantee that she will suddenly wake up, see you and instinctively alter to starboard, leaving you even worse placed than before.

- **Stage 3**. The stand-on vessel *must* act when she 'finds herself so close that a collision cannot be avoided by the action of the give-way vessel alone'.

Stage 2 is considered optional by the Rules (in reality it is anything but – the only choice that you make is when and how to manoeuvre). Stage 3 is mandatory. More importantly, the Rules allow you to act 'as soon as it becomes apparent' that the give-way vessel is not taking appropriate action: if you wish, you can make a move early – before the situation gets out of hand.

When the stand-on vessel should alter course:

Standing on and waiting for the other vessel to alter is scary, and I would always advocate caution, at an early stage, over the nail-biting bravado of those who stand on regardless. It is difficult to give general advice about when and how to alter – each case is different. But you will find yourself getting progressively more uneasy as the range closes. At some stage, the decision to make a move in accordance with Rule 17 becomes irresistible. In my experience, this point is considerably too late: I would invariably prefer to start the escape manoeuvre well before it gets too exciting!

You really should not ever be in the position where you have allowed the situation to get to Stage 3 but if you do, you will just have to judge matters by the seat of your pants. Good luck: tell me about it in the bar one of these days!

Do not forget that you also have the option of five or more short blasts on the whistle, and you could also call the other vessel on VHF Channels 16 or 13.

5

Getting close to another vessel

I have found that there are two very reliable indicators for when I get too close to another vessel: you can see the navigation lights reflected in the water (as long as it isn't too rough), and you can hear the other ship's machinery noise.

You will make up your own mind, but for me, these indicators pretty much define the limit of my comfort zone in a yacht, and they are well inside my comfort zone in a big ship.

The Retiring Turn and the Chicken Circle

In any action to avoid a collision, there are a range of manoeuvres at your disposal by varying course and speed. In the past, I have found two 'escape manoeuvres' helpful in clearing the air and removing doubt in the other vessel's mind – particularly at short ranges. These are the 'Retiring Turn' and the 'Chicken Circle'. Both are designed to reduce the closing rate and give you more time to react. You can also choose whether or not to reduce speed during the turn, and on which course to steady up.

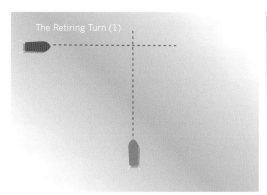

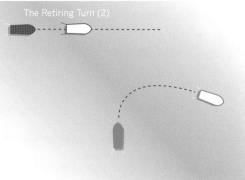

Red, the give-way vessel does not appear to be taking appropriate action to avoid a collision. What action should the green vessel take?

Green alters away and slows down on a slightly opening course.

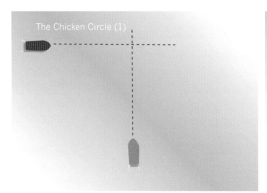

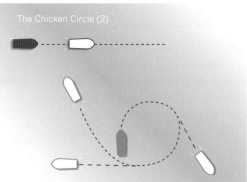

Red, the give-way vessel does not appear to be taking appropriate action to avoid a collision. What action should the green vessel take?

Green alters away in a full circle, slowing down if necessary, giving time for the red vessel to get past and clear. Green can come out of the circle on a variety of courses.

Part 2: Rules for vessels in restricted visibility (Rule 19)

This is one area where the theory is actually quite straightforward: there are just three rules that apply in restricted visibility. The practice, however, is altogether more complex, and proficiency comes largely through time on the bridge and hard-won experience.

Before we start, however, don't forget your fog signals which should be made: 'in or near an area of Restricted Visibility, whether by day or night' (*Rule 35*).

First Rule

Rule 19(b)

Every vessel shall proceed at a safe speed adapted to the prevailing circumstances and conditions of restricted visibility. A power-driven vessel shall have her engines ready for immediate manoeuvre.

The circumstances and conditions relating to safe speed are set out in Rule 6. The speed, that is, beyond which a vessel cannot be confident of being *able to take proper and effective action to avoid a collision* and *stopped within a distance appropriate to the prevailing circumstances and conditions*.

All vessels – including sailing boats – should make sure that they have manoeuvring power available at short notice in restricted visibility. This is not the place for bravado: you may well need your engines to get you out of harm's way. Personally, when I'm out in my yacht I always start the motor in fog; it may reduce my ability to hear fog signals, but significantly increases the boat's manoeuvrability.

Second Rule

Rule 19(d)

A vessel that detects by radar alone the presence of another vessel shall determine if a close-quarters situation is developing and/or risk of collision exists. If so, she shall take avoiding action in ample time, provided that when such action consists of an alteration in course, so far as possible the following shall be avoided:

(i)   An alteration of course to port for a vessel forward of the beam, other than for a vessel being overtaken;

(ii) An alteration of course toward a vessel abeam or abaft the beam.

In this context I would draw your attention to two important elements of Rule 7:

1   That you should not make assumptions on scanty information, particularly scanty radar information, and

2   That if you are in any doubt at all about whether or not a risk of collision exists, you should assume that it does.

You always have the option of speeding up or slowing down, but essentially the manoeuvring instructions of this rule boil down to the need to alter to starboard in all cases except when a vessel is on your starboard quarter (see attached diagram). You will notice that the Rules assume that you will wish to take action no matter where the other vessel is approaching you from: there is no such thing as a stand-on vessel in restricted visibility (Guiding Principle 3).

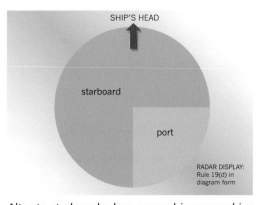

Alter to starboard when a vessel is approaching from any direction other than the starboard quarter. Alter to port when a vessel is approaching from this quadrant.

Note that this is the *only* radar diagram in this book aligned to ship's head: all others will be aligned to North with a display that is assumed to be compass-stabilised.

In making the adjustments in course that this rule suggests, bear in mind that a slight alteration in course and speed will be almost imperceptible to another ship observing on radar. Make the turns significant and chunky if navigation and other traffic allow. You might even turn right away to reduce the closing rate if necessary.

Two examples, both of which assume a compass – stabilised display.

Example 1

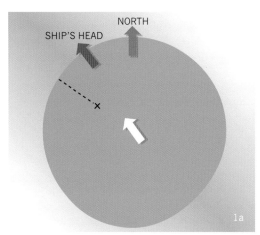

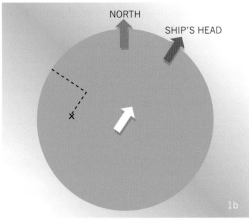

Assume a compass stabilised display. Contact approaching from the port bow. You need to alter course to starboard.

You have altered course to starboard: contact tracking down your port side.

Example 2

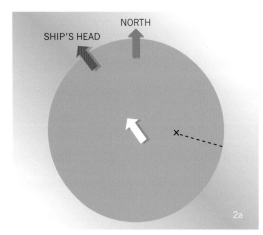

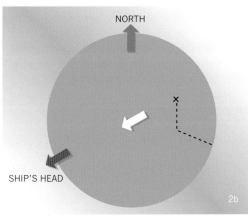

Contact approaching from the starboard quarter. You need to alter course to port.

You have altered course to port and the other vessel will track by to the east.

Third Rule

Rule 19(e)

Except where it has been determined that a risk of collision does not exist, every vessel that hears apparently forward of her beam the fog signal of another vessel, or which cannot avoid a close-quarters situation with another vessel forward of her beam, shall reduce her speed to be the minimum at which she can be kept on her course. She shall if necessary take all her way off and in any event navigate with extreme caution until danger of collision is over.

If you haven't got radar and you hear a fog signal which appears to originate ahead of you; or if you cannot rule out the fact that a risk of collision might exist; or if a close-quarters situation is inevitable – then you must reduce to the minimum speed to maintain steerage way. Or even just stop. I can't say it enough: you must be very, very careful in fog (or any other form of reduced visibility). It is a dangerous place to be and ultimately the best protection is to reduce the closing rate either by altering course or be reducing speed.

Overtaking: In addition to these three rules, remember that the overtaking rule only applies when you can see the other vessel. In poor visibility, you can never be certain that other vessels know where you are, or your precise orientation.

Narrow Channels and Fairways, and Separation Schemes: Additional rules for narrow channels and fairways, and those for separation schemes, which apply in all conditions of visibility, are covered in Chapter 6.

5

Chapter 5 – Self-test (Rules 8, 11–19)

1. a. When two sailing vessels can see each other and are approaching, with the wind on opposite sides, who stands on and who gives way? (*Rule 12(a)(i).*)
   b. When 2 sailing vessels can see each other and one is overtaking the other, who stands on and who gives way? (*Rule 13(a).*)

2. Complete Rule 13(b):
   A vessel shall be deemed to be overtaking when coming up with a another vessel from a direction more than _____ degrees abaft her beam, that is, in such a position with reference to the vessel she is overtaking, that at night she would be able to see only _____ the of that vessel but neither of her sidelights.

3. Two power-driven vessels in sight of each other are approaching from head-on. What action should they each take? (*Rule 14(a).*)

4. a. Two power-driven vessels in sight of each other are approaching each other in a crossing situation. One can see the other's green navigation light, and the other can see the first vessel's red navigation light. Who gives way?
   b. What should the give-way vessel avoid doing if the circumstances of the case admit? (*Rule 15.*)

5. Complete Rule 16:
   Every vessel which is directed to keep out of the way of another vessel shall, so far as possible, take _____ and _____ to keep well clear.

6. a. What, in general, should the stand-on vessel do? (*Rule 17(a)(i).*)
   b. When *may* the stand-on vessel act to avoid a collision? (*Rule 17(a)(ii).*)
   c. When *must* the stand-on vessel act? (*Rule 17(b).*)

7. Name the four categories of vessel that a power-driven vessel must keep out of the way of. (*Rule 18 (a).*)

8. A vessel engaged in fishing meets a vessel Restricted in her Ability to Manoeuvre. Each vessel can see the other and there is a risk of collision. Who has to give way? (*Rule 18(c)(ii).*)

9. Complete Rule 19(a):
   This Rule applies to vessels not in sight of one another when navigating _____ or _____ an area of Restricted Visibility.

10. If, in restricted visibility, you detect by radar a vessel closing you on a steady bearing from 70 degrees on the starboard bow, what direction of manoeuvre should you avoid if possible? (*Rule 19(d)(i).*)

6 Narrow Channels and Fairways, and Separation Schemes: *Rules 9 and 10*

Read through Rules 9 and 10 before you start on this chapter.

I have brought the discussion on Narrow Channels and Fairways, and on Separation Schemes into a separate chapter because the Rules that apply in these busy and congested waterways are hugely important to the mariner. They also apply in all states of visibility, and are overlaid on the standard Manoeuvring Rules. They may complicate life a little, but they undoubtedly succeed in their principal objective of making navigation in these busy and often stressful areas as well-regulated and as safe as possible.

The regulations for Narrow Channels and Fairways, and for Separation Schemes are similar but not identical. For instance, crossing vessels must not impede the passage of vessels which can only navigate safely within a narrow channel or fairway, whereas in a Separation Scheme a crossing vessel (whilst it might try not to impede through traffic) is not bound so to do by the Rules.

Narrow Channels and Fairways (Rule 9)

It is not too easy to define the terms 'narrow channel' or 'fairway'. A 'narrow channel' is – well – pretty much what it says on the tin: a stretch of water, used as a shipping channel, which is narrow in relation to the size or volume of shipping that uses it. The term 'fairway' refers to a more open stretch of water, normally buoyed and often dredged to a specific depth, which may form the outer approaches to a port. Suffice it to say that large vessels operating in certain channels or fairways, like the approaches to many harbours, will often go aground if they move outside the marked channel. And smaller vessels will do so in commensurately smaller waterways. Rule 9 is written to protect the interests of vessels which can safely navigate only within the confines of that waterway.

Many ships in this situation will hoist the shape and lights of a vessel constrained by its draught, but as we have already established, this is not mandatory. (*Rule 28.*)

Rule 9 applies in any condition of visibility – including restricted visibility (when the efficient use of radar for collision avoidance will be of paramount importance).

Specifically **in a narrow channel or fairway** (and the first of these is by far the most important):

- **Crossing vessels, sailing vessels and vessels less than 20 metres in length must not** *impede* **any vessel that can navigate safely only within that channel, no matter which side you are approaching from and irrespective of the nature of the two vessels involved.** The word 'impede' is used deliberately. It only appears in Rule 9, 10 and 18, putting an onus on the 'not-to-impede vessel' to take early action to prevent a risk of collision from developing, without relieving either vessel of its ultimate responsibility for collision avoidance. See Rule 8(f).

- Fishing vessels may fish in a narrow channel or fairway – but, if it chooses to do so, it must not impede **any other** vessel navigating in the channel.

- When navigating along a narrow channel or fairway, you must keep as far to the right as you can. This is just good sense in a narrow channel with two-way traffic.

- Wherever possible, avoid anchoring in a narrow channel of fairway.

- If a vessel restricted to a narrow channel is in doubt over the intentions of a crossing vessel, it may sound five or more short blasts on its whistle.

- A vessel approaching a bend in a narrow channel where an approaching vessel might be obscured should sound a single prolonged blast (4–6 seconds) on the whistle as it approaches. This signal must be answered by any vessel approaching the bend from the other side.

- And finally, the overtaking rule still applies **when vessels are in sight of each other**. However, because of the geography, a set of sound signals have been established (*Rule 34(c)(i)*) to clarify the intentions of both vessels when 'the vessel to be overtaken has to take action to permit safe passage [of the overtaking vessel].' (*Rule 9(e)(i)*.) (See Chapter 4.)

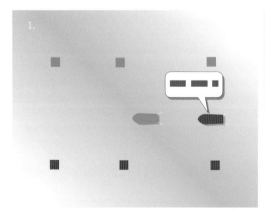

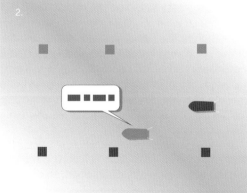

The red vessel wants to overtake the green vessel, passing to starboard, and needs the green vessel's co-operation to do so . . .   . . . so it makes the appropriate sound signal.

The green vessel is content; it moves to the port side of the channel and signals its agreement.

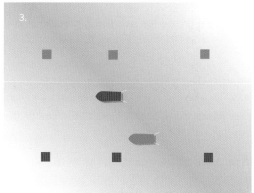

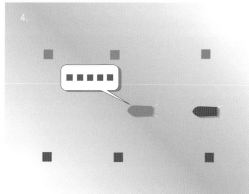

6

And the red vessel overtakes.

If the green vessel is not content, it makes 5 short blasts.

Negotiating narrow channels and fairways

These are waters which will almost certainly be subject to local regulations and, no matter what size or nature of vessel you are navigating, you need to be aware of the regulations, the relevant Vessel Traffic Scheme and its controlling VHF frequency, and any extant notices to mariners. This applies to small boats as well as large ships: in the approaches to Southampton Water, for instance, the harbour authority establishes a moving 'Precautionary Area' around large vessels moving along the channel, with pretty stiff fines for anyone who contravenes the regulations.

Separation Schemes (Rule 10)

Rule 10 also applies in any condition of visibility. The critical bit of this rule lies in the second line. It reads:

'This Rule applies to traffic Separation Schemes adopted by the organisation *and does not relieve any vessel of her obligation under any other Rule*.'

In other words, Rule 10 sets out special provisions for the use of Separation Schemes, but all of the standard collision avoidance rules still apply, whether a ship is following the Scheme, crossing a lane, or pursuing any other activity. A ship following the Scheme, in other words, is still obliged to give way to vessels approaching her from the starboard side. However, fishing vessels, sailing vessels and vessels of less than 20 metres in length are *not to impede* vessels following a traffic lane[1]: they are required to take early action to avoid getting in the way of the through traffic. But if they miscalculate, and a risk of collision does materialise, the normal rules *do* apply.

---

[1]This is subtly different from the rules for a narrow channel or fairway where fishing vessels, sailing vessels, vessels of less than 20 metres **and crossing vessels** are not to impede the safe passage of vessels within the channel.

A **Traffic Separation Scheme** is little more than a maritime motorway, with **Traffic Lanes** divided by a **Separation Lines** or a **Separation Zone**, designed to separate the two contrary traffic flows. This framework is drawn in magenta on the chart, with arrows to indicate the direction of traffic flow.

Large vessels on passage through the Scheme are obliged to use the traffic lanes – and would be barking mad not to. Occasionally a 'rogue vessel' is reported by the Dover Coastguard going the wrong way through the Dover Separation Scheme – which quite simply constitutes one of the most dangerous and reckless acts that you can undertake on the high seas.

Often, particularly in narrow straits, you will find an '**Inshore Traffic Zone**' outside the boundaries of the Scheme itself, principally for the use of inshore shipping. Rule 10(d) is quite specific about its use – and it is not there to provide an alternative route through the Scheme for large vessels.

Rule 10(d)

(i)   A vessel shall not use an inshore traffic zone when she can safely use the appropriate traffic lane within the adjacent traffic separation scheme. However, vessels of less than 20 metres in length, sailing vessels and vessels engaged in fishing may use the inshore traffic zone.

(ii)   Notwithstanding subparagraph (d)(i), a vessel may use an inshore traffic zone when en route to or from a port, offshore installation or structure, pilot station or any other place situated within the inshore traffic zone, or to avoid immediate danger.

Like motorways, you are discouraged from doing anything in a Separation Scheme that would interfere with the safe and free flow of traffic. So:

- You must use the appropriate lane and stick to the general direction of flow defined by the lane (*Rule 10(b)*). If you are not intending to use the Scheme, you should avoid it by as wide a margin as possible (*Rule 10(h)*).

- You must not – as far as possible – intrude into or cross the central reservation (the Traffic Separation Line or Separation Zone). Only four categories of vessel allowed to enter a Separation Zone:

  - Crossing vessels

  - A vessel joining or leaving a lane

  - In an emergency, to avoid immediate danger

  - A vessel engaged in fishing.

- Vessels Restricted in their Ability to Manoeuvre when engaged in operations for the **maintenance and safety of navigation**, and those engaged in **laying, servicing or picking up a submarine cable** are exempted from complying with Rule 10 if necessary in the course of their work.

- If you can possibly avoid it, don't anchor inside a Separation Scheme or close to its ends. By implication, this also applies to stopping in the water, although it is not explicitly mentioned in Rule 10.

- Join and leave at the start of the Separation Lane if possible. If not, ease in or out of the flow at as small an angle as you can manage.

- Only cross the Scheme if you have to. And if it is necessary, do so on a **heading** 90 degrees from the direction of flow. In other words, you should predominantly steer a course at right angles to the traffic, recognising that the effects of the tidal stream may well set you on an oblique track.

- If you aren't using the Scheme, keep well clear of it. Through traffic will probably want to stay more in the centre of the lanes than on the edge in order to maintain adequate separation[2].

Separation schemes

Not all Separation Schemes are frantically busy; some are effectively used as way-points for organising through traffic. However, I have always rather enjoyed negotiating the busier lanes, not least the Straits of Dover. My advice would be to:

- Make sure that you are up-to-date on radio navigational warnings.

- Monitor the right VHF frequency.

- Watch closely for crossing traffic, particularly ferries, and for small craft. Take action early to avoid close quarters situations if you can.

- Be especially vigilant for slow but inexorable closing rates with the shipping that you are close to.

- And finally, as any good seaman would, think ahead: always be aware of your freedom of manoeuvre – and take any necessary steps to maximise your available sea room.

---

[2]Compare this with the rule for narrow channels (Rule 9(a)) which encourages vessels in narrow channels to stay as far to the starboard side as possible.

And Finally

The International Code signal 'YG' means **'You appear not to be complying with the traffic separation scheme'**. If you see this, be certain to check both your own movements and those of ships in your immediate area.

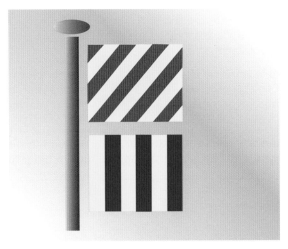

International Code: 'YANKEE GOLF'
"You appear not to be complying with the traffic separation scheme."

Chapter 6 – Self-test (Rules 9 and 10)

1. What vessels are required not to impede the passage of a vessel which can safely navigate only within a narrow channel or fairway? (*Rule 9(b)*, (c) and (d).)

2. What sound signal should a vessel make when approaching a bend in a narrow channel where approaching vessels might be obscured? (*Rule 9(f), 34(e).)*

3. Are vessels allowed to anchor in a narrow channel? (*Rule 9(g)*.)

4. a. If you want to overtake a vessel in a narrow channel, and you are in sight of each other, what signal do you make?
   b. What should she reply if she is happy to take the necessary action to permit you to pass?
   c. What sound signal does she make if she is not happy? (*Rule 9(e)(i)*.)

5. Complete Rule 9(a):
   A vessel proceeding along the course of a narrow channel or fairway shall keep as near to the _____ _____ of the channel or fairway which lies on her _____ _____ as is safe and practicable.

6. If you have to cross a traffic lane in a Separation Scheme, what heading should you try to adopt? (*Rule 10(c)*.)

7. In Rule 10(d)(i) and (ii), there are a number of types of vessel and activities which would justify using an Inshore Traffic Zone. How many can you name? (A tough question – but see how well you can do.)

8. A similar but easier question: what are the four categories of vessel that can enter a Separation Zone? (*Rule 10(e)*.)

9. What two classes of vessel must not impede the passage of vessels following a traffic lane? (*Rule 10(i) and (j)*.)

10. And the final question. There are two classes of vessel that are exempted from complying with Rule 10 to the extent necessary to carry out their work. What are they? (*Rule 10(k) and (l)*.)

6

7 Some examples of Collision Avoidance

Here are a few examples: none has a 'set' answer because in any encounter you must judge your response in the light of the circumstances in which you find yourself.

1. Head-on encounter between two power-driven vessels (Rule 14)

Two power-driven vessels, approaching each other head-to-head.

Rule 14

(a) When two power-driven vessels are meeting on reciprocal or nearly reciprocal courses so as to involve risk of collision each shall alter her course to starboard so that each shall pass on the port side of the other.

(b) Such a situation shall be deemed to exist when a vessel sees the other ahead or nearly ahead and by night she could see the masthead lights in line or nearly in line and/ or both sidelights and by day she observes the corresponding aspect of the other vessel.

(c) When a vessel is in any doubt as to whether such a situation exists she shall assume that it does exist and act accordingly.

One or both vessels alter course to starboard, and sound one short blast.

Don't mess around with niceties here: this is when two vessels have the highest closing rate, and the two skippers the least time to think. Even if you are only approximately head-to-head, turn to starboard if it is safe to do so, sound one short blast and clear out. The greatest effect that you can have is to turn onto a course that is at right angles to the other vessel's course: clearly, this is only necessary if she is very close, or you think that she has not seen you.

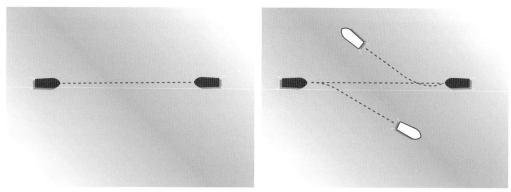

Two power-driven vessels approaching each other, head-on.

7

2. Power-driven vessels crossing. You are the give-way vessel (Rules 15, 16 and 17)

Rule 15

When two power-driven vessels are crossing so as to involve risk of collision, the vessel which has the other on her own starboard side shall keep out of the way and shall, if the circumstances of the case admit, **avoid crossing ahead of the other vessel**.

Rule 16

Every vessel that is directed to keep out of the way of another vessel shall, so far as possible, **take early and substantial action to keep well clear**.

Rule 17

(a)

    (i)   Where one of two vessels is to keep out of the way of **the other shall keep her course and speed.**

    (ii)   The latter vessel may however take action to avoid collision by her manoeuvre alone, as soon as it becomes apparent to her that the vessel required to keep out of the way is not taking appropriate action in accordance with these Rules.

(b) When, from any cause, the vessel required to keep her course and speed finds herself so close that collision cannot be avoided by the action of the give-way vessel alone, she shall take such action as will best aid to avoid collision.

continued

(c) A power-driven vessel which takes action in a crossing situation in accordance with sub-paragraph (a)(ii) of this Rule to avoid collision with another power-driven vessel shall, if the circumstances of the case admit, not alter course to port for a vessel on her own port side.

(d) This Rule does not relieve the give-way vessel of her obligation to keep out of the way.

A Consideration

If you are not keen to lose too much ground, you could try coming round to point a judicious distance behind the other vessel's stern, and continuously adjust your heading to maintain this offset as he passes by. When he crosses your original track you carry on as you were before. That way, he will be in no doubt that you have seen him, and you will pass comfortably astern of him.

Just remember the traffic lights: if you can see the other vessel's **green light** you stand on. If you can see her **red light**, you have to give way to her. If you have to give way, do it early and in a way that is unlikely to confuse the other vessel. Virtually always the correct action for the give-way vessel will be to turn to starboard in order to avoid passing ahead of the other vessel.

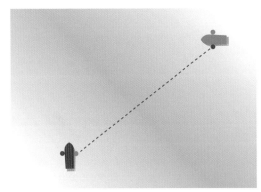 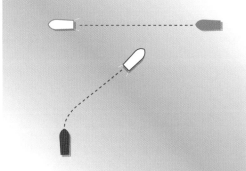

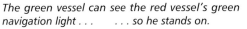

The green vessel can see the red vessel's green navigation light . . .   . . . so he stands on.   *One short blast and alter course to starboard.*

3. Power driven vessels crossing in sight of each other (you are the stand-on vessel) and the other vessel does not give way. (Rule 17(a)(ii) and (b))

7

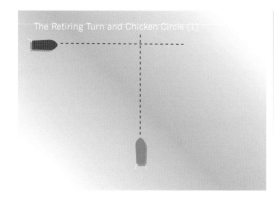

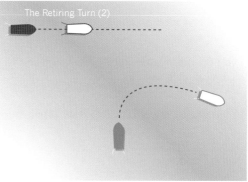

Green alters away and slows down on a slightly opening course.

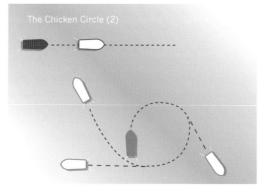

Green alters away in a full circle, slowing down if necessary, giving time for the red vessel to get past and clear. Green can come out of the circle on a variety of courses.

Your actions will depend entirely on the circumstances: I have portrayed two options here which are explained more fully in Chapter 5, but there is quite a lot more you could do, either in isolation or in combination.

- You may just stop
- You could make five short blasts
- You could call him on VHF

The one thing that you probably won't want to do, however, is to turn to port unless there are very good reasons to do so. If, once you are committed to a turn to port, the other vessel suddenly wakes up and decides to go to starboard (as she should), you will be very much worse placed than before.

Giving way late is actually a pretty common occurrence, particularly when the stand-on vessel is relatively small and inconspicuous. The Rules, however, allow the stand-on vessel to make an early move, and if the situation continues to deteriorate, you are **obliged** to manoeuvre when you find yourself so close that a collision cannot be avoided by the action of the give-way vessel alone.

If you do alter course, remember to make the manoeuvring sound signals. In this instance they will be valuable.

4. You are overtaking another vessel. (Rule 13)

Rule 13

(a) Notwithstanding anything contained in the Rules of Part B, Sections I and II, any vessel overtaking any other shall keep out of the way of the vessel being overtaken.

(b) A vessel shall be deemed to be overtaking when coming up with a another vessel from a direction more than 22.5 degrees abaft her beam, that is, in such a position with reference to the vessel she is overtaking, that at night she would be able to see only the sternlight of that vessel but neither of her sidelights.

(c) When a vessel is in any doubt as to whether she is overtaking another, she shall assume that this is the case and act accordingly.

(d) Any subsequent alteration of the bearing between the two vessels shall not make the overtaking vessel a crossing vessel within the meaning of these Rules or relieve her of the duty of keeping clear of the overtaken vessel until she is finally past and clear.

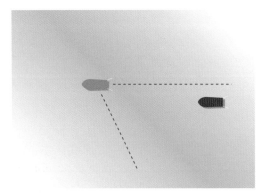

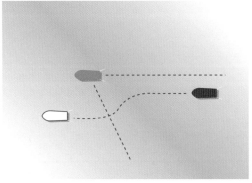

The red vessel is approaching from more than 22 ½ degrees abaft the green vessel's beam, and the 2 vessels can see each other . . . . . . so red is the 'overtaking vessel'.

Alter to one side, making the appropriate sound signal (in this case 2 short blasts) and remain clear until finally past and clear.

You may alter either way to pass the other vessel, making the appropriate sound signal of one or two short blasts (except in a narrow channel where the signals are different). You must recognise that, once you have started the overtaking manoeuvre, you remain under an obligation to keep clear of the other vessel, irrespective of her subsequent movements, until you are **'finally past and clear'**. The vessel being overtaken, however, is under no obligation to maintain course and speed.

The 'overtaking rule' applies whenever vessels are in sight of each other – in open water, narrow channels and separation lanes. It also applies to every form of vessel, including sailing vessels and those with reduced manoeuvrability. It only applies when vessels can see each other.

5. Sail and power. (Rule 18(a))

You are in a 30-foot sailing boat under sail, crossing the English Channel from England to France, and threading you way across the east-going shipping lane, outside the Channel Separation Schemes. A power-driven vessel is approaching you on a steady bearing from your starboard side. You know that Rule 18(a) requires power-driven vessels to keep out of the way of sailing vessels, and you know that Rule 17(a)(i) invites the stand-on vessel to keep her course and speed. What action should you take?

Rule 18(a)

Except where Rule 9, 10, and 13 otherwise require:

(a) A power-driven vessel under way shall keep out of the way of:

   (i) A vessel Not Under Command;

   (ii) A vessel Restricted in her Ability to Manoeuvre;

   (iii) A vessel Engaged in Fishing;

   (iv) A sailing vessel.

Rule 17(a)(i)

   (i) Where one of two vessels is to keep out of the way of the other shall *keep her course and speed.*

This is a sort of Clint Eastwood moment: '. . . *you've got to ask yourself one question: Do I feel lucky?'* When the chips are down, a fully manoeuvrable power-driven vessel in good visibility must keep clear of any sailing vessel, except when being overtaken by it. In practice, however, a small sailing vessel would be well advised to take early and positive action to avoid a close-quarters situation from developing with any large power driven vessel. You just cannot rely on the fact that a big ship can or will take avoiding action – or even that she has seen you in the first place.

Avoiding a Close-Quarters Situation

I would advise against a small sailing boat pushing its luck and putting itself in a situation where it would embarrass large ships. In the absence of any other considerations, and if it was safe to do so, I would probably alter at about 4–5 miles, point a sensible distance astern of the oncoming vessel (a large enough alteration to be visible from his bridge), and track his stern as he comes past.

For what it's worth, my advice would be the same whether the smaller vessel was being propelled by sail or power.

Under sail, you are under no obligation to make a sound signal.

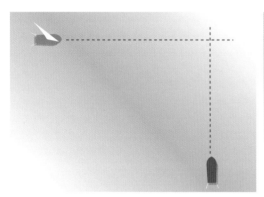

The sailing boat (green) has the power driven vessel (red) on a steady bearing.

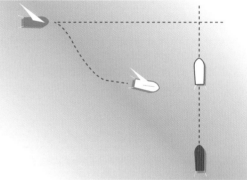

Green may decide to avoid a close quarters situation developing by making an early alteration to pass astern of the red vessel.

6. Crossing a Separation Lane where there is an appreciable tidal stream. (Rule 10(c))

You need to cross a Separation Lane, but there is a strong tidal stream running: what course to you steer?

Rule 10(c)

(c) A vessel shall so far as practicable avoid crossing traffic lanes, but if obliged to do so shall cross on a heading as nearly as practicable at right angles to the general direction of traffic flow.

Rule 10(c) is pretty clear: you should keep your **heading** 'as nearly as practical at right angle to the general direction of traffic flow'. You will undoubtedly have to do a fair amount of ducking and weaving to get between the shipping, and sometimes it's a bit like a tortoise trying to cross a motorway: the task involves a high level of stress and your acceleration may not always be up to the job. For that reason, you should make your 'default' heading 90 degrees to the line of traffic flow, which gives you the highest crossing rate, and gets you across in the shortest time – but you will have to steer whatever course is necessary for collision avoidance. It's not for the faint-hearted.

It does, inevitably, mean that you will be swept down-tide, and you need to take this into account in your planning. Don't try to 'crab' into the tide, particularly in a slow-moving vessel. Other ships will just find your movements confusing.

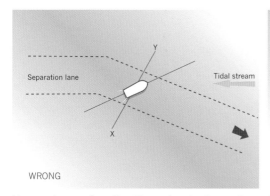

WRONG

You need to get from X to Y, crossing the Separation Scheme with a strong westerly tide running . . . . . . Do not be tempted to 'crab' into the tidal stream to maintain your track.

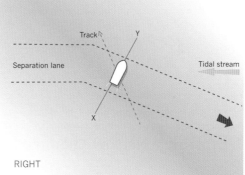

RIGHT

Instead, maintain your track at 90° to the flow of traffic where possible . . . . . . And accept that you will be offset to the west.

7. You Meet Crossing Traffic In a Separation Lane. (Rule 10)

You are proceeding through a Separation Scheme in your bulk carrier and you meet a cross-channel ferry approaching at high speed from your starboard side. What action do you take?

You will recall that vessels of 20 metres or less in length, sailing and fishing vessels should not impede the safe passage of a power-driven vessel following a traffic lane. (*Rule 10(i) and (j)*.) Larger vessels, however, suffer no such restraint, although in my experience most ferries that cross busy and crowded waterways do their best to avoid interfering with the through traffic.

If you find yourself in this situation, you may need all the flexibility you can muster. The reaction time is likely to be short; you may well be navigationally constrained in strong tidal streams, with a lot of adjacent traffic. You are, however, obliged to take action and give way to a vessel approaching from your starboard side. The answer may well be a combination of course and speed alterations, carefully judged to cause minimal interruption to other shipping but which will have the desired effect on the bearing rate of the crossing vessel.

You could try making early contact with the other vessel on VHF, and you would certainly want to make manoeuvring sound signals as you get closer.

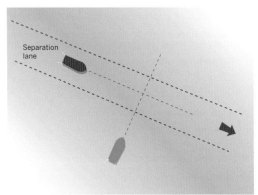 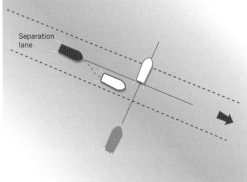

You are proceeding down the Separation Lane, and have a ferry on a steady bearing to starboard. . . .

Combination of course and speed alteration to pass under the crossing vessel's stern.

8. Crossing a Narrow Channel. Rule 8(b)

You need to cross a Narrow Channel, but a large vessel is moving along the channel.

Rule 9(d)

(d) A vessel shall not cross a narrow passage or fairway if such crossing impedes the passage of a vessel which can safely navigate only within such channel or fairway. The latter vessel may use the sound signal prescribed in Rule 34(d) if in doubt as to the intention of the crossing vessel.

This situation is all about the word **'impede'**. Vessels that are **'not to impede'** are free to manoeuvre, provided that they do not interfere with the safe passage of the other vessel. In the case of a narrow channel or fairway, it is crossing vessels, vessels less than 20 metres in length, sailing and fishing vessels that must not impede the passage of a vessel that can only navigate safely within the channel.

This is not a difficult issue: you need to wait until you can cross without getting under the feet of the larger ship.

How do you know that the ship is constrained to remain in the channel? Because it will – or at least it should – be showing the lights or shape for a Vessel Constrained by its Draught (a cylinder or three red all-round lights in a vertical line). (*Rule 28.*)

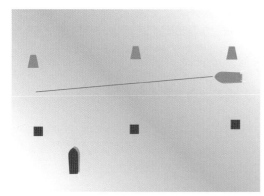 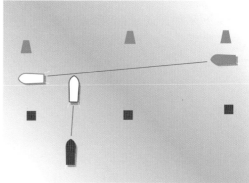

The red vessel wants to cross a narrow channel, but a large vessel (green) is already committed to it. The red vessel must wait outside the channel until he can cross without impeding the green vessel.

Green is now past, so the red vessel may cross without impeding green's passage.

If everyone in the world was sensible, this would work like a dream. They aren't though. And if you find yourself in the position of the green vessel, constrained by your draught to remain in the channel, it can sometimes be a little nerve-racking. Stand on – but trust no one. You can always sound five short blasts on the siren if you are worried by another vessel (if nothing else, it helps relieve some of the tension) and you should never overlook the usefulness of VHF. But your options are undoubtedly limited – and you just have to use your judgment and experience to give yourself as much time and manoeuvring space as you can.

I can't urge small boat users strongly enough to keep well clear of vessels constrained by their draught. Their lights are easy enough to make out, although their shapes often aren't – but you will recognise them when you see them. You should avoid impeding their safe passage and, where possible, stay out of their way completely.

9. Approaching a blind corner in a narrow channel. (Rules 9(f) and 34(e))

You are in a narrow Norwegian fjord, approaching a blind corner. What do you do next?

Rule 9(f)

(f)   A vessel nearing a bend or an area of a narrow channel or fairway where other vessels may be obscured by an intervening obstruction shall navigate with particular alertness and caution and shall sound the appropriate signal prescribed in Rule 34(e).

continued

7

Rule 34(e)

(e) A vessel nearing a bend or an area of a channel or fairway where other vessels may be obscured by an intervening obstruction shall sound one prolonged blast. Such signal shall be answered with a prolonged blast by any approaching vessel that may be within hearing around the bend or behind the intervening obstruction.

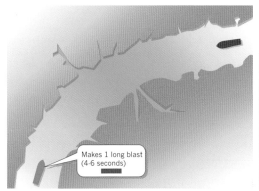

Ship approaching a blind corner in good visibility.

This rule applies to all vessels, not just to power driven vessels. You make one prolonged blast (4–6 seconds) on the whistle and wait to hear whether it has been reciprocated by a vessel on the other side of the bend. Even if you don't hear a reply, you should still **'navigate with particular alertness and caution'**, take up a position on the starboard side of the channel, look for a good passing place . . . and breathe in.

If you are in a small vessel and you hear this sound, and it is quite common, my advice would be to clear the channel as quickly as possible to provide room for the big ship to pass.

When the ships can see each other, if one of them is in any doubt about the other's intentions, it should make five short blasts on the siren. (*Rule 34(d)*.)

10. Meeting a tow. (Rule 3(g)(vi))

Rule 3(g) (partial)

(g) The term 'vessel Restricted in her Ability to Manoeuvre' means a vessel which from the nature of her work is restricted in her ability to manoeuvre as required by these Rules and is therefore unable to keep out of the way of another vessel.

　　(vi) A vessel engaged in a towing operation such as severely restricts the towing vessel and her tow in their ability to deviate from their course.

Unless a tow declares itself to be Restricted in its Ability to Manoeuvre, because it is '. . . **severely restricted** . . . **In its ability to deviate from its course,**' it is expected to behave like any other power-driven vessel for collision avoidance. Which is simple enough. Anyone who has spent time towing a big ship, however, will know that it is rather like watching an elephant tap-dance: slow, ponderous and absorbing. Good seamanship in the unencumbered vessel would dictate that, where possible, it should take early action to avoid a close-quarters situation from developing.

So, for the unencumbered vessel:

- If at all possible, as the stand-on vessel, do not force the tow to give way to you. Take early action to keep out of her way.
- However, if the tow is not RAM, it is obliged to react as a power driven vessel, taking any appropriate action to avoid a collision.
- If the tow has declared itself to be RAM, you must keep clear.

And for the tow:

- If not RAM, react as a normal power-driven vessel. Recognising that the tow will almost certainly slow down your ability to manoeuvre, you will need to start reacting early.
- If you are RAM, stand on and watch the situation unfold.

In restricted visibility, a tow is accorded no special privileges, whether it is RAM or not.

11. Meeting a vessel that is Restricted in its Ability to Manoeuvre. (Rule 3(g)(vi))

You are in a container ship and you see, on your port bow at five miles, two military vessels steaming along side-by-side, clearly involved in underway replenishment. You can also see Restricted in its Ability to Manoeuvre shapes on both ships. The bearing is steady. How do you manoeuvre?

Rule 8(a) – (e)

(a) Any action to avoid collision shall be taken in accordance with the Rules of this Part and shall, if the circumstances of the case admit, be positive, made in ample time and with due regard to the observance of good seamanship.

(b) Any alteration of course and/or speed to avoid collision shall, if the circumstances of the case admit be large enough to be readily apparent to another vessel observing visually or by radar; a succession of small alterations of course and/or speed shall be avoided.

continued

(c) If there is sufficient sea room, alteration of course alone may be the most effective action to avoid a close-quarters situation provided that it is made in good time, is substantial and does not result in another close-quarters situation.

(d) Action taken to avoid collision with another vessel shall be such as to result in passing at a safe distance. The effectiveness of the action shall be carefully checked until the other vessel is finally past and clear.

(e) If necessary to avoid collision or allow more time to asses the situation, a vessel may slacken her speed or take all way off by stopping or reversing her means of propulsion.

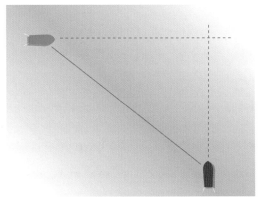

There are a lot of options here, all of which involve keeping out of the way of the vessels Restricted in their Ability to Manoeuvre. You are probably not going to want to alter to port unless you can do so unambiguously early.

Alternatively, you could slow down substantially (speeding up and passing across the bow would probably be quite an adventurous decision).

And finally, you could come round to starboard, possibly slowing down in the process and either parallel her course or conduct a 'chicken turn' to starboard.

Vessel Restricted in its Ability to Manoeuvre. Vessels closing on a steady bearing.

12. Two sailing vessels meeting on opposite tacks. (Rules 12(a) and 12(b))

Rule 12(a)(i) and 12(b)

(a) When two sailing vessels are approaching one another, so as to involve risk of collision, one of them shall keep out of the way of the other as follows:

   (i) When each of them has the wind on a different side, the vessel which has the wind on the port side shall keep out of the way of the other;

(b) For the purposes of this Rule the windward side shall be deemed to be the side opposite to that on which the mainsail is carried or, in the case of a square rigged vessel, the side opposite to that on which the largest fore-and-aft sail is carried.

The give-way vessel is the one which has the wind coming from her port side – the vessel on the port tack, in other words.

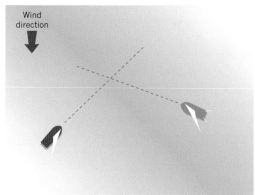

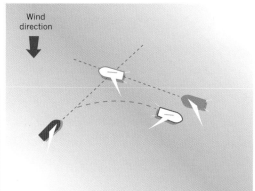

The red vessel is on the PORT TACK and must give way. The green vessel is on the STARBOARD TACK and should stand on.

The red vessel, which is on the port tack, alters to starboard to avoid a collision with the green vessel, which is on the starboard tack.

It is courteous for the give-way vessel to pass down-wind of the stand-on vessel, but the course of action will depend entirely on the circumstances. The skipper of the stand-on vessel traditionally stands in the cockpit of his yacht, shaking his fist and shouting **'STARBOARD!'** at the top of his voice. Meanwhile, the skipper of the give-way boat stands defiantly in his cockpit, staring at the other boat and muttering **'IDIOT!'** under his breath. It's all a lot of fun.

Sailing vessels are not obliged to make manoeuvring sound signals.

The most important thing when sailing, and particularly when close-hauled, is to keep a reliable lookout, including under and behind the sails, and always remembering to look out astern. If you react early, you will probably be able to get away with just a minor alteration of course, and without the need to adjust your sails significantly (but you will of course miss out on the opportunity to shout at the other boat!.

13. Two sailing vessels meeting on the same tack. (Rule 12(a)(ii))

Rule 12(a)(ii)

(a)   When two sailing vessels are approaching one another, so as to involve risk of collision, one of them shall keep out of the way of the other as follows:

   (ii)   When both have the wind on the same side, the vessel which is to windward shall keep out of the way of the vessel which is to leeward.

The leeward vessel – the one that is more close-hauled – stands on.

The other needs to adjust its course to keep clear. Again, there are a number of options, and the best course of action will depend on the circumstances. She may choose to pass astern of the other vessel, to come round and parallel her, or indeed to come right round and tack.

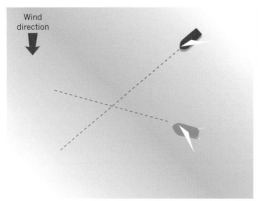

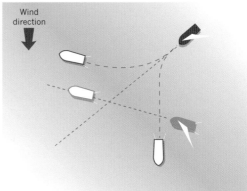

Both vessels are on the STARBOARD tack, but the green vessel is to leeward . . . so red must give way.

Red may either come round parallel to green's course or pass astern of her.

14. Restricted visibility. Vessel closing on radar (1). (Rule 19(d))

Rule 19(d)

(d) A vessel that detects by radar alone the presence of another vessel shall determine if a close-quarters situation is developing and/or risk of collision exists. If so, she shall take avoiding action in ample time, provided that when such action consists of an alteration in course, so far as possible the following shall be avoided:

  (i) An alteration of course to port for a vessel forward of the beam, other than for a vessel being overtaken;

  (ii) An alteration of course toward a vessel abeam or abaft the beam.

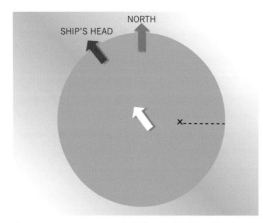

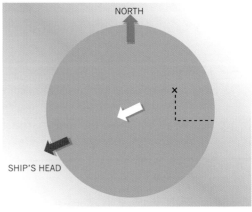

Assume a compass stabilised display. Contact approaching from the starboard quarter.

With the other vessel closing from your starboard quarter, make a generous alteration of course to port.

The radar in these illustrations is compass stabilised, north up.

You detect a vessel on radar closing from your starboard quarter. It must therefore be moving faster than you and converging on your track.

Bear in mind that the overtaking rule does not apply in restricted visibility: if you could see the other vessel it would probably apply here, but in fog you cannot be certain that the other vessel has detected you, and you must always take responsibility for collision avoidance yourself.

In this case, you might alter course boldly to port, navigation and other shipping permitting. You do not, of course, make manoeuvring sound signals in restricted visibility when you are not in sight of each other since they would be easy to confuse with fog signals.

15. Restricted visibility. Vessel closing on radar (2). (Rule 19(d))

For this vessel on your starboard bow to be on a steady bearing, you must be fairly broad on her port bow. Manoeuvring in restricted visibility is not really a time for half-measures: you might choose to turn substantially to starboard (navigation and shipping permitting) to put her on your port bow and driving his bearing down your port side.

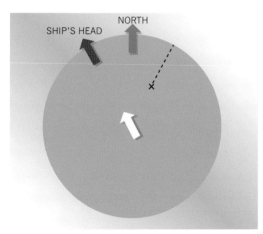

Assume a compass stabilised display. Contact approaching from the starboard.

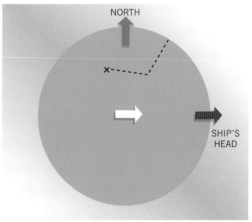

With the other vessel closing from your starboard bow, alter firmly to starboard and put him on your port bow.

16. Restricted visibility. No operational radar. Foghorn heard. (Rule 19(e))

Rule 19(e)

(e) Except where it has been determined that a risk of collision does not exist, every vessel that hears apparently forward of her beam the fog signal of another vessel, or which cannot avoid a close-quarters situation with another vessel forward of her beam, shall reduce her speed to be the minimum at which she can be kept on her course. She shall if necessary take all her way off and in any event navigate with extreme caution until danger of collision is over.

If you hear another foghorn **abaft your beam**, keep going and try to work out whether it is getting louder or fainter, drawing right or left. You might consider adjusting your heading to some extent to give yourself greater separation, but slowing down or stopping will only increase the closing rate, and is unlikely to be helpful.

If, without an operational radar, you hear a foghorn **forward of your beam**, and you cannot be absolutely certain that it is **not** a problem, you should slow down to the minimum speed for maintaining steerage way. If you really are worried, just stop (keeping your engines available for immediate manoeuvre). Rule 7(c) warns that: 'assumptions shall not be made on the basis of scanty information, especially scanty radar information.' And having no radar in fog leaves you with pretty scanty information! So take it very carefully indeed.

Direction of the prevailing flow of shipping

In fog, it is always worth knowing the direction of the prevailing flow of shipping. If you are really worried, one option that you might consider is to turn away from the foghorn and steady up on a course that is parallel to the general direction of traffic in that area, which may reduce the closing rate of at least some of the shipping.

Always maintain directional control of your vessel if you can. It is often better to keep moving, with control over your heading, than to lie stopped in the water.

8 Particular Issues for Yachts and Small Boats

Manoeuvring Rules for boats less than 20 metres in length, in good visibility

In Open Water (for example. when crossing the English Channel)

- A prudent small vessel will take early action to avoid the risk of a collision. If risk of collision does exist, however, the standard rules apply.

Crossing a Separation Lane

- Any vessel less than 20 metres in length or a sailing boat should **avoid impeding** the safe passage of a power driven vessel following a traffic lane. If, however, risk of collision does exist, the standard rules will apply.

Passage through a Separation Scheme

- Vessels of less than 20 metres in length, together with sailing vessels and vessels engaged in fishing may (and probably should) use the Inshore Traffic Zone.

Crossing a Narrow Channel or Fairway, or navigating along it

- Crossing vessels, together with any vessel less than 20 metres in length or a sailing boat, should **avoid impeding** the safe passage of a vessel which can navigate safely only within the narrow channel or fairway. If, however, risk of collision does exist, the standard rules will apply.

Lights and Shapes

Lights and shapes are there to help vessels identify each other, and to help other mariners work out what a vessel is doing. To that end, it is really important that small boats, which are inconspicuous and don't always conform to a set pattern like so much commercial shipping, carry the right lights, that the lights work, and that they are properly visible and not obscured by obstructions.

A few tips for small boat users:

- Always check and service your navigation lights over the winter. Make sure that you carry spares.

- Periodically check that your lights are visible over the right arcs, and that they are not obstructed. The best way of doing this is to switch the lights on and walk or row round the boat to look at them. Significantly, the inquiry into the sinking of the yacht OUZO reported that, while all the navigation lights were in working order, their luminosity was badly degraded due to crazing. One commentator installed a crazed bow light filter into his boat and reported a loss of 60–75 per cent in brightness and range.

- Before setting out on a voyage, check that your navigation lights work. Have a system of rechecking them periodically during the voyage.

- When you change from sail to power and back again your light configuration changes. Don't be idle – make sure that you do it.

- You can sometimes use discretion over the anchor ball. If you anchor in an area that is likely to be used by other craft on passage it is undoubtedly worth raising it, but if you are tucked away in a secluded anchorage, it is perhaps more discretionary.

- However an anchor light is pretty much essential. It helps other people coming into the anchorage at night to know where you are. And you never know when you will need it to guide you back from the pub!

Sailing boat lights (Rule 25)

At night or in restricted visibility, a sailing vessel must show sidelights and a sternlight.

If **less than 20 metres** in length, it may amalgamate these three lights into a sectored 'combined lantern' at or near the top of the mast, where it can best be seen.

If **less than 7 metres** in length, it should, if possible, show one or other of these light combinations. If not, you should have at hand a torch or lantern with a white light that can be used to prevent a collision. (But don't rely on a torch unless it is absolutely essential: install proper navigation lights if you can.)

In addition to the side and sternlights, a sailing vessel when under way may show two all-round masthead lights, red over green, but not if it is using a combined lantern. In practice, I have only ever seen large sailing vessels showing the red over green at the masthead, where it provides a very distinctive signal. You don't, however, see it very often.

The combined lantern should not be used when under power, when it will show above the steaming light: this is very confusing for other mariners.

A sailing vessel, under way and sailing. Sidelights and sternlight only – no masthead light.

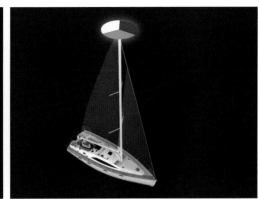

A sailing vessel less than 20 metres in length, under way and sailing. The single combined lantern at the masthead.

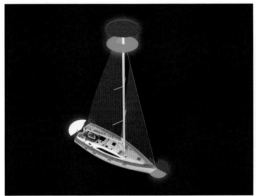

Sailing vessel under way. Sidelights and a sternlight, together with red over green all-round lights at the masthead.

A sailing vessel less than 50 metres in length propelling itself by power.

Sailing vessel under way, less than 7 metres in length.

Motor boats and sailing boats under power (Rule 23)

Assuming that you are not one of the fortunate few who own a motor boat greater than 50 metres in length[1] (in which case you will almost certainly be employing a professional skipper to take care of these tiresome details on your behalf), you will need the following lights on your boat:

- Masthead light
- Sternlight
- Sidelights

A power driven vessel, less than 50m in length, under way.

However, **if the boat is less than 12 metres in length**, you may show:

- All-round white light (masthead light and sternlight combined).
- Sidelight

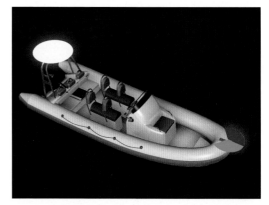

A power driven vessel less than 12 metres in length.

Finally, **if your vessel is less than 7 metres in length, and cannot exceed 7 knots** in speed you may show:

- An all-round white light
- Where practical: sidelights.

[1]Clearly, if your boat is over 50 metres in length, you will need two masthead steaming lights.

A power driven vessel less than 7 metres in length and capable of less than 7 knots.

> ### Invest in sidelights
>
> Even in a slow, small boat (less than 7 metres in length) I would most strongly advise you to show sidelights. We mariners are not telepathic and if you want any assistance in collision avoidance, you have to give us a bit of help. Sidelights are generally neither difficult nor expensive to fit and they help enormously.

Vessels under oars (Rule 25(d)(ii))

A vessel under oars is, from the perspective of the Rules, treated like a sailing vessel of equivalent size. The very great majority of vessels that are powered by oars, and used at night, are the tenders to private yachts, and they should carry a hand torch (I usually supplement this with a head-torch) which 'shall be exhibited in sufficient time to prevent collision'.

When you are using your dinghy under power at night, it should be lit as a power-driven vessel of less than 7 metres in length, and should show a single white all-round light with, if possible, sidelights.

A vessel propelled by oars.

Small boats at anchor and aground (Rule 30 (e) & (f))

Vessels less than 7 metres in length, when anchored clear of narrow channels, fairways, anchorages or any other navigation route, are not required to show anchor lights or shapes.

Vessels less than 12 metres in length, when aground, need not show specific shapes or lights for a vessel aground. I have no doubt, though, that your friends will still find out before long!

Visibility of lights in small boats (Rule 22)

Vessel 12–50 metres in length:

- Masthead light: 5 miles (3 miles if vessel less than 20 metres in length)
- Sidelight: 2 miles
- Sternlight: 2 miles

Vessel less than 12 metres in length:

- Masthead light: 2 miles
- Sidelight: 1 miles
- Sternlight: 2 miles

Shapes to carry on your yacht

If you are fitting out a super-yacht, you will probably need the full suite of shapes and lights.

However, you only need two shapes on a small sailing boat: a black ball and a black cone. And for a motor boat – just a black ball.

A sailing boat with sails hoisted, but which is nevertheless under power should, by day, show a black cone apex downwards.

When at anchor, the black ball should be hoisted by day, in the fore part of the vessel, and where it can best be seen.

In vessels greater than 20 metres in length (Annex I para 6):

- Diameter of the ball should be not less than 0.6 metres
- Base diameter of the cone should be not less than 0.6 metres

In smaller vessels the shapes can be commensurately smaller.

And finally, don't forget your foghorn

There is just one piece of advice that I have for anyone buying a foghorn for a small boat:

THE LOUDER THE BETTER!

A sound that is embarrassingly loud in the chandlery is often no more than a rather sad grunt at sea. The only reason to buy a foghorn and to give it a home for months on end is that so it can be heard when you want it to be heard. That is its sole purpose in life, and if it can't even manage that, it doesn't deserve to be onboard. If it is aerosol powered, make sure that you carry a few spare canisters (and try to remember where you stowed them).

9 Buoyage

What you need to know about buoys: they aren't complicated, but they are an essential tool for maintaining the spatial awareness that you need when deciding how to manoeuvre for traffic in restricted waters.

Buoys are a country's way of welcoming you to their waters. There are never enough of them, but they are used to mark the safe channels in and out of harbour, and around obstructions. The first thing to remember about buoys is that they are never in a precise spot: they are anchored to the bottom, often with more than one anchor, but it is not unknown for them to drag their anchors. And even when they aren't dragging, the slack in their mooring chains allows the buoy to describe a small circle on the surface of the water, so visual fixing using a buoy as one of the fixing points is unlikely to be particularly reliable.

On the other hand, buoys are seldom very far out of position, even when they have dragged a bit. Consequently, when the navigator of a yacht (or a ship) pops up to report that the buoy 'has clearly been removed' or that it's 'in the wrong place', the wise skipper will take a long hard look at the navigation – just to be certain.

There are two sorts of buoyage in general use:

- The **cardinal system** (yellow and black buoys and marks), where marks are designed to indicate which direction a danger lies in, and therefore which direction is safe for navigation.
- The **lateral system** (green and red buoys and marks), which is commonly used in navigable channels, with one set of shapes and colours being left to one side, and the other set on the other side.

The cardinal system is applied consistently around the world and does not change. By contrast, there are two similar but distinct forms of lateral buoyage, both of which have been sanctioned by the International Association of Lighthouse Authorities (IALA).

- **Region B** applies to North and South America, Korea, Japan and the Philippines.
- **Region A** applies to all countries in the world that do not fall into Region B.

Buoys can be identified by a number of features: their shape and the shape of their topmark; the name which is generally painted on the side; their lights, sound signals, colour and (occasionally) a radar transponder.

In addition, there are three other kinds of navigational buoys and marks:

- Safe water marks
- Isolated danger marks
- Special marks

They too have their own special characteristics.

The Cardinal System

The clever thing about the cardinal system is that you don't need to know where you are, or even what harbour you are going into in order to remain safe.

In essence, the system uses the four cardinal points of the compass (north, south, east and west) to mark an obstruction. The buoys in each quadrant can be distinguished from each other by colour, topmark and light characteristics. Thus, a 'northerly cardinal mark' lies generally to the north of an obstruction, and vessels should pass to the north of it. Not all cardinal marks are buoys. There are a lot of beacons too – but they all share the same colouring, topmarks and lights so that every single cardinal mark will fit into the one system.

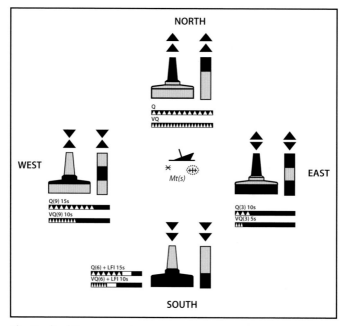

The Cardinal Buoyage system.

Recognising Cardinal Marks. The topmarks are the key to recognising cardinal buoys and beacons. The north and south topmarks point north and south respectively.

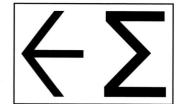

The easterly topmark forms a primitive 'E' and the westerly topmark a side-on 'W'.

In a rather quaint way, the colour scheme, too, is linked to the topmark: all cardinal buoys and beacons are painted black and yellow, and the cones of the topmark always point towards the 'black bits' of the paint scheme.

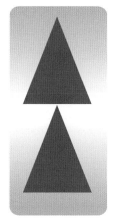

Northerly cardinal buoy. Painted black at the top.

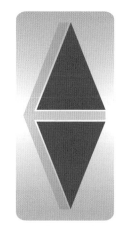

Easterly cardinal buoy. Painted black at the top and bottom.

Westerly cardinal buoy. Painted black in the middle.

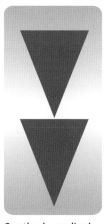

Southerly cardinal buoy. Painted black at the bottom.

As you might expect, the lights also follow a fairly predictable pattern. They are organised around the clock face and are all either Quick or Very Quick Flash (White). So:

Easterly cardinal	Q or VQ (3)
Southerly cardinal	Q or VQ (6) followed by a long flash (in case you lost count)
Westerly cardinal	Q or VQ (9)
Northerly cardinal	Continuous Q or VQ

The buoys themselves

EAST CARDINAL

Topmark: Looks a bit like a primitive 'E' with black shading between the horizontals.

Colours: Following the system, this mark is yellow in the middle and black at the top and bottom.

Light: This mark is placed at 3 o'clock from the obstruction and so has a group of 3 flashes.

SOUTH CARDINAL

Topmark: Points south (reasonably enough).

Colours: Same system as before: the topmarks always point to the 'black bits' so the buoy is painted with yellow on the top and black at the bottom.

Light. Sitting at 6 o'clock, this buoy gives 6 flashes. However, recognising the mental limitations of most mariners, the designers thought (quite correctly) that it would be too easy to confuse the 6 flashes of the south marker with the 9 flashes of the west mark, so they put a long flash at the end of the southerly mark's 6 quick flashes.

WEST CARDINAL

Topmark: Shaped like a 'W' that has been rotated through 90°. It is also sometimes said to look like a **Wineglass**.

Colours: Same system again. The black is in the centre with yellow at the top and bottom.

Light. This is the 9 o'clock buoy and gives 9 straight flashes.

9

NORTH CARDINAL

Topmark: Both cones point north.

Colours: Same system again. Black at the top and yellow at the bottom.

Light. This is the 'midnight buoy' and flashes continuously.

THE LATERAL SYSTEM

IALA System A

IALA System A is the system that is used throughout Europe, and much of the rest of the world, with the exception of North and South America, Korea, Japan and Philippines. The buoys can be distinguished by colour, topmark, light and also by shape, depending on which side they are to be passed.

In a nutshell when you are sailing **WITH THE FLOOD TIDE**, you leave the red buoys and marks to port, and the green buoys and marks to starboard. The direction of the main flood stream is generally fairly simple to determine, but where there is any ambiguity, it is indicated on the chart by a hollow magenta arrow.

Lateral marks

Direction of buoyage symbol

Port hand buoys and marks:

- Can-shaped
- Have cylindrical top-marks
- Are painted red
- Have red lights
- Have even numbering

Starboard hand buoys:

- Conical in shape
- Have triangular top-marks
- Are painted green
- Have green lights
- Have odd numbering

9

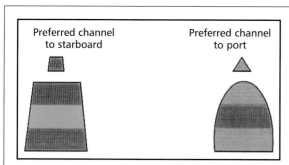

Modified Lateral Marks

These are the 'preferred channel marks', used when a channel marked by cardinal buoyage divides. You can pass either side, but one side is favoured. Personally, I can never recall seeing these buoys at sea.

9

IALA System B

Used in North and South America, Korea, Japan and the Philippines.

System B is actually very similar to System A, except that you keep the red buoys to starboard when entering harbour, and the green buoys to port. The universal mnemonic for this is:

'RED – RIGHT – RETURNING'

Lateral marks

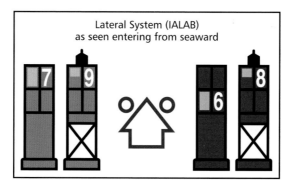

Port hand buoys and marks:

- Are painted green
- Square-shaped
- Have odd numbering
- Have green lights

Starboard hand buoys:

- Are painted red
- Buoys can be slant-sided ('nun-buoys')
- Have even numbering
- Have red lights

9

Preferred channel to starboard (when entering harbour)	Preferred channel to port (when entering harbour)
• May have a green light • May be lettered	• May have a red light • May be lettered

Modified Lateral Marks

These are the opposite colours and shapes to IALA System A.

Safe Water Marks

These are common to every buoyage system. A safe water mark has navigable water all round it and is often used as the outer marker to a conventional buoyage system, or as a mid-channel marker.[1]

Topmark: Circular, red

Colour: Red and white vertical stripes

Light: A gentle rhythm: this is a 'safe buoy'. Isophase or occulting, or one long flash every 10 seconds. May also show the Morse 'A' (•–).

Isolated Danger Mark

These too are common to every buoyage system. They mark an isolated danger of small area that has navigable water all round it.

Topmark: Two black balls

Colour: A sinister red and black in horizontal stripes.

Light: Group flashing white (2).

---

[1] I am grateful to Joe Haines of the Exmouth branch of the RNLI Lifeguards for permission to use this photograph.

Special marks

These are not specifically intended as aids to navigation, but instead they are marker buoys for some feature that will almost always be charted. In the Solent, for instance, the great majority are racing marks: spherical yellow buoys, each with a unique name, unlit and often with no topmark.

Topmark: Yellow diagonal cross (if any)

Colour: Yellow, usually with the name painted in black

Light: Yellow (when fitted)

Shape: Any shape that does not conflict with navigation buoys.

Chapter 9 – Self-test (Buoyage)

1. What colours, lights and topmark does a westerly cardinal buoy display?

2. a. In Western Europe, when entering a harbour, on which side would you expect to keep the red buoys?

   b. How would that change in the United States?

   c. What chart symbol is used to show the direction of buoyage?

3. a. When is an Isolated Danger Mark used?

   b. What colour, light and topmark does it display?

4. a. When is a Safe Water Mark used?

   b. What colour, light and topmark does it display?

5. What is a Modified Lateral Mark?

6. You are lost and you see this buoy: which side of it should you pass, and what light would you expect it to show?

10 Distress Signals: *Annex IV*

10

Take a few moments to read through Annex IV of the Rules before you start this chapter.

Every book that I have ever read about survival at sea describes a moment when the survivors see a ship that passes close by without spotting them and then disappears over the horizon, leaving them alone on a vast, empty ocean. There is a moral here about keeping a good lookout, but it also shows why the Rules go to so much trouble to define a variety of signals that can be used in a whole range of circumstances to convey just one unambiguous message:

'I am in distress and I need assistance'.

Pretty much wherever you are, you **should** be able to get your message across.

I'm going to bang on a little here: the signals laid out at Annex IV are **DISTRESS SIGNALS**, no more and no less. They are not to be used for any other purpose; they will never convey any other meaning; and the only people who will use them are people who need to be rescued. Distress signals do not, **under any circumstances**, mean 'I have a box of time-expired flares that I am shooting off to celebrate my wife's birthday.' If you see them, or if you hear them, they are for real.

We all know 'SOS' and most of us know the Morse equivalent: '● ● ● — — — ● ● ●'. Quite a lot of people are aware of 'MAYDAY', but did you realise that the first signal – a gun fired at intervals of about one minute – was a distress signal? Or that the continuous sounding of a fog-signalling apparatus means something more important than 'I have a particularly dreadful four-year old aboard.' You need to be aware of **all** of these signals, and I have always found that trying to recall the full list of 15 signals is a pleasantly virtuous way of passing the long night watches.

There is one last aspect of emergency signals that I need to raise, and that is the use of mobile phones. Of course, in an emergency, I would use any available means of getting my message across, including a mobile phone. But as any mariner knows, mobile phones work perfectly until you are a few miles offshore, and then they go quiet. And to me, that doesn't count as a reliable bit of safety equipment. Of course, if you are in range and you have a good signal, no one would criticise you for using it, but it is not a substitute for 'proper' emergency equipment, like VHF, flares, and so on.

There are 15 distress signals set out in the Rules. You really need to know them all. I have put them on a separate page so that, if you wish, you can copy the list and use it for reference.

10

MARITIME DISTRESS SIGNALS (Annex IV to the Rules)

1. A gun or other explosive signal fired at intervals of about one minute.

2. A continuous sounding with any fog-signalling apparatus.

3. Rockets or shells, throwing red stars, fired one at a time, at short intervals.

4. A signal made by radiotelephony or by any other signalling method consisting of the group '●●● — — — ●●●' (SOS) in Morse Code.

5. A signal sent by radiotelephony consisting of the spoken word 'MAYDAY'.

6. The International Code Signal of distress indicated by NC.

7. A signal consisting of a square flag having above it or below it a ball, or anything resembling a ball.

8. Flames on the vessel (as from a burning tar barrel, oil barrel, etc)

9. A rocket parachute flare or a hand flare showing a red light.

10. A smoke signal giving off orange-coloured smoke.

11. Slowly and repeatedly raising and lowering arms outstretched to each side.

12. The radiotelegraph alarm signal. (Twelve four-second dashes per minute, set at one-second intervals.)

International Code: 'NOVEMBER CHARLIE'
"I am in distress, and need assistance."

13. The radiotelephone alarm signal. (Alternate tones of 1300Hz and 220Hz transmitted on 2182kHz for a period of 30–60 seconds.)

14. Signals transmitted by emergency position-indicating radio beacons (EPIRB).

15. Approved signals transmitted by radio communications systems, including survival craft radar transponders.

NB. 'The use or exhibition of any of the foregoing signals, except for the purposes of indicating distress and the need of assistance, and the use of other signals which may be confused with any of the above signals is prohibited.'

11 International Marine VHF Channels as used in the UK

Unless otherwise instructed, use **Channel 16** for initial calling since it should be monitored by all ships and authorities. Bear in mind, however, that its principal purpose is for **DISTRESS AND SAFETY** communications. Never block it, or use it for idle chatter. If you use it for an initial call, swap to a working channel as soon as you make contact.

Use **Channel 13** as the principal channel for inter-ship safety and navigation. If you get no joy on Channel 16 with another vessel, it may be worth trying Channel 13.

Channel 70 is exclusively for DSC calling for safety and emergency communications, and must not be used for any other purpose.

Around the UK coast

Primary inter-ship working channels:	06, 08, 09, 10, **13,** 15, 17, 69, 72, 73, 77
UK Coastguard uses:	10, 23, 67, 84, 86
UK Marinas use:	80 or M1 (37)
UK Yacht Clubs use:	M1 (37) or M2

In other countries, these designations may differ, although the use of Channels 16, 70 and 13 are consistent. See www.navcen.uscg.gov/marcomms/vhf.htm for the list of channel allocations in US waters.

Note: the British government has advised against relying on VHF communications for collision avoidance, although when operating in a Vehicle Traffic Service (VTS) area the use of VHF is often mandatory. This is quite sensible: the Rules themselves are sufficient and adequate to keep you safe. And VHF, even if you can get through, is often beset by poor reception, imperfect understanding and the need to make sure that you are speaking to the person who you think he is. It undoubtedly has value, and use it when it will add value, but don't lean on it too heavily.

12 The Rules – Verbatim

The full text of the International Regulations for the Prevention of Collisions at Sea 1972, with subsequent changes to November 2003, is set out below.

Part A – General

Rule 1: *Application*

(a) These Rules shall apply to all vessels upon the high seas and in all waters connected therewith navigable by seagoing vessels.

(b) Nothing in these Rules shall interfere in the operation of special rules made by an appropriate authority for roadsteads, harbours, rivers, lakes or inland waterways connected with the high seas and navigable by seagoing vessels. Such special rules shall conform as closely as possible to these Rules.

(c) Nothing in these Rules shall interfere with the operation of any special rules made by the Government of any State with respect to additional station or signal lights or shapes or whistle signals for ships of war and vessels proceeding under convoy, or with respect to additional station or signal lights, or shapes for fishing vessels engaged in fishing as a fleet. These additional station or signal lights, shapes or whistle signals shall, so far as possible, be such that they cannot be mistaken for any light, shape, or signal authorized elsewhere under these Rules.

(d) Traffic Separation Schemes may be adopted by the Organization for the purpose of these Rules.

(e) Whenever the Government concerned shall have determined that a vessel of special construction or purpose cannot comply fully with the provisions of any of these Rules with respect to number, position, range or arc of visibility of lights or shapes, as well as to the disposition and characteristics of sound-signalling appliances, such vessel shall comply with such other provisions in regard to number, position, range or arc of visibility of lights or shapes, as well as to the disposition and characteristics of sound-signalling appliances, as her Government shall have determined to be the closest possible compliance with these Rules in respect to that vessel.

Rule 2: *Responsibility*

(a) Nothing in these Rules shall exonerate any vessel, or the owner, master, or crew thereof, from the consequences of any neglect to comply with these Rules or of the neglect of any precaution which may be required by the ordinary practice of seamen, or by the special circumstances of the case.

(b) In construing and complying with these Rules due regard shall be had to all dangers of navigation and collision and to any special circumstances, including the limitations of the vessels involved, which may make a departure from these Rules necessary to avoid immediate danger.

Rule 3: *General Definitions*

For the purpose of these Rules, except where the context otherwise requires:

(a) The word "vessel" includes every description of watercraft, including non-displacement craft, WIG craft and seaplanes, used or capable of being used as a means of transportation on water.

(b) The term "power driven vessel" means any vessel propelled by machinery.

(c) The term "sailing vessel" means any vessel under sail provided that propelling machinery, if fitted, is not being used.

(d) The term "vessel engaged in fishing" means any vessel fishing with nets, lines, trawls, or other fishing apparatus which restrict manoeuvrability, but does not include a vessel fishing with trolling lines or other fishing apparatus which do not restrict manoeuvrability.

(e) The word "seaplane" includes any aircraft designed to manoeuvre on the water.

(f) The term "vessel not under command" means a vessel which through some exceptional circumstance is unable to manoeuvre as required by these Rules and is therefore unable to keep out of the way of another vessel.

(g) The term "vessel restricted in her ability to manoeuvre" means a vessel which from the nature of her work is restricted in her ability to manoeuvre as required by these Rules and is therefore unable to keep out of the way of another vessel.

The term "vessel restricted in her ability to manoeuvre" shall include but not be limited to:

(i) A vessel engaged in laying, servicing, or picking up a navigational mark, submarine cable or pipeline;

(ii) A vessel engaged in dredging, surveying or underwater operations;

(iii) A vessel engaged in replenishment or transferring persons, provisions or cargo while underway;

(iv) A vessel engaged in the launching or recovery of aircraft;

(v) A vessel engaged in mine clearance operations;

(vi) A vessel engaged in a towing operation such as severely restricts the towing vessel and her tow in their ability to deviate from their course.

(h) The term "vessel constrained by her draft" means a power-driven vessel which because of her draft in relation to the available depth and width of navigable water is severely restricted in her ability to deviate from the course she is following.

(i) The word "underway" means a vessel is not at anchor, or made fast to the shore, or aground.

12

(j)   The words "length" and "breadth" of a vessel mean her length overall and greatest breadth.

(k)   Vessels shall be deemed to be in sight of one another only when one can be observed visually from the other.

(l)   The term "restricted visibility" means any condition in which visibility is restricted by fog, mist, falling snow, heavy rainstorms, sandstorms and any other similar causes.

(m) The term "Wing-in-Ground (WIG) craft" means a multi-modal craft which, in its main operational mode, flies in close proximity to the surface by utilising surface-effect action.

Part B – Steering and Sailing Rules

Section I – Conduct of Vessels in any Condition of Visibility

Rule 4: *Application*

Rules in this section apply to any condition of visibility.

Rule 5: *Look-out*

Every vessel shall at all times maintain a proper look-out by sight and hearing as well as by all available means appropriate in the prevailing circumstances and conditions so as to make a full appraisal of the situation and of the risk of collision.

Rule 6: *Safe Speed*

Every vessel shall at all times proceed at a safe speed so that she can take proper and effective action to avoid collision and be stopped within a distance appropriate to the prevailing circumstances and conditions.

In determining a safe speed the following factors shall be among those taken into account:

(a)   By all vessels:

(i)   The state of visibility;

(ii)   The traffic density including concentrations of fishing vessels or any other vessels;

(iii) The manoeuvrability of the vessel with special reference to stopping distance and turning ability in the prevailing conditions;

(iv)   At night the presence of background light such as from shore lights or from back scatter from her own lights.

(v)   The state of wind, sea and current, and the proximity of navigational hazards;

(vi)   The draft in relation to the available depth of water.

(b)   Additionally, by vessels with operational radar:

(i)   The characteristics, efficiency and limitations of the radar equipment;

(ii)   Any constrains imposed by the radar range scale in use;

(iii) The effect on radar detection of the sea state, weather and other sources of interference;

(iv)   The possibility that small vessels, ice and other floating objects may not be detected by radar at an adequate range;

(v)   The number location and movement of vessels detected by radar;

(vi)   The more exact assessment of the visibility that may be possible when radar is used to determine the range of vessels or other objects in the vicinity.

Rule 7: *Risk of Collision*

(a) Every vessel shall use all available means appropriate to the prevailing circumstances and conditions to determine if risk of collision exists. If there is any doubt such risk shall be deemed to exist.

(b) Proper use shall be made of radar equipment if fitted and operational, including long-range scanning to obtain early warning of risk of collision and radar plotting or equivalent systematic observation of detected objects.

(c) Assumptions shall not be made on the basis of scanty information, especially scanty radar information.

(d) In determining if risk of collision exists the following considerations shall be among those taken into account:

   (i) Such risk shall be deemed to exist if the compass bearing of an approaching vessel does not appreciably change;

   (ii) Such risk may sometimes exist even when an appreciable bearing change is evident, particularly when approaching a very large vessel or a tow or when approaching a vessel at close range.

Rule 8: *Action to Avoid Collision*

(a) Any action to avoid collision shall be taken in accordance with the Rules of this Part and shall, if the circumstances of the case admit, be positive, made in ample time and with due regard to the observance of good seamanship.

(b) Any alteration of course and/or speed to avoid collision shall, if the circumstances of the case admit be large enough to be readily apparent to another vessel observing visually or by radar; a succession of small alterations of course and/or speed shall be avoided.

(c) If there is sufficient sea room, alteration of course alone may be the most effective action to avoid a close-quarters situation provided that it is made in good time, is substantial and does not result in another close-quarters situation.

(d) Action taken to avoid collision with another vessel shall be such as to result in passing at a safe distance. The effectiveness of the action shall be carefully checked until the other vessel is finally past and clear.

(e) If necessary to avoid collision or allow more time to asses the situation, a vessel may slacken her speed or take all way off by stopping or reversing her means of propulsion.

(f)

   (i) A vessel which, by any of these rules, is required not to impede the passage or safe passage of another vessel shall when required by the circumstances of the case, take early action to allow sufficient sea room for the safe passage of the other vessel.

   (ii) A vessel required not to impede the passage or safe passage of another vessel is not relieved of this obligation if approaching the other vessel so as to involve risk of collision and shall, when taking action, have full regard to the action which may be required by the rules of this part.

   (iii) A vessel the passage of which is not to be impeded remains fully obliged to comply with the rules of this part when the two vessels are approaching one another so as to involve risk of collision.

12

12

Rule 9: *Narrow Channels*

(a) A vessel proceeding along the course of a narrow channel or fairway shall keep as near to the outer limit of the channel or fairway which lies on her starboard side as is safe and practicable.

(b) A vessel of less than 20 meters in length or a sailing vessel shall not impede the passage of a vessel which can safely navigate only within a narrow channel or fairway.

(c) A vessel engaged in fishing shall not impede the passage of any other vessel navigating within a narrow passage or fairway.

(d) A vessel shall not cross a narrow passage or fairway if such crossing impedes the passage of a vessel which can safely navigate only within such channel or fairway. The latter vessel may use the sound signal prescribed in Rule 34(d) if in doubt as to the intention of the crossing vessel.

(e)

    (i) In a narrow channel or fairway when overtaking can take place only if the vessel to be overtaken has to take action to permit safe passing, the vessel intending to overtake shall indicate her intention by sounding the appropriate signal prescribed in Rule 34(c)(i). The vessel to be overtaken shall, if in agreement, sound the appropriate signal prescribed in Rule 34(c)(ii) and take steps to permit safe passing. If in doubt she may sound the signals prescribed in Rule 34(d).

    (ii) This rule does not relieve the overtaking vessel of her obligation under Rule 13.

(f) A vessel nearing a bend or an area of a narrow channel or fairway where other vessels may be obscured by an intervening obstruction shall navigate with particular

alertness and caution and shall sound the appropriate signal prescribed in Rule 34(e).

(g) Any vessel shall, if the circumstances of the case admit, avoid anchoring in a narrow channel.

Rule 10: *Traffic Separation Schemes*

(a) This rule applies to traffic separation schemes adopted by the Organization and does not relieve any vessel of her obligation under any other rule.

(b) A vessel using a traffic separation scheme shall:

    (i) Proceed in the appropriate traffic lane in the general direction of traffic flow for that lane.

    (ii) So far as is practicable keep clear of a traffic separation line or separation zone.

    (iii) Normally join or leave a traffic lane at the termination of the lane, but when joining or leaving from either side shall do so at as small an angle to the general direction of traffic flow as practicable.

(c) A vessel shall so far as practicable avoid crossing traffic lanes, but if obliged to do so shall cross on a heading as nearly as practicable at right angles to the general direction of traffic flow.

(d)

    (i) A vessel shall not use an inshore traffic zone when she can safely use the appropriate traffic lane within the adjacent traffic separation scheme. However, vessels of less than 20 meters in length, sailing vessels and vessels engaged in fishing may use the inshore traffic zone.

    (ii) Notwithstanding subparagraph (d)(i), a vessel may use an inshore traffic zone when en route to or from a port, offshore installation or structure, pilot station or any other place situated within the inshore traffic zone, or to avoid immediate danger.

(e) A vessel, other than a crossing vessel or a vessel joining or leaving a lane shall not normally enter a separation zone or cross a separation line except:

   (i) In cases of emergency to avoid immediate danger;

   (ii) To engage in fishing within a separation zone.

(f) A vessel navigating in areas near the terminations of traffic separation schemes shall do so with particular caution.

(g) A vessel shall so far as practicable avoid anchoring in a traffic separation scheme or in areas near its terminations.

(h) A vessel not using a traffic separating scheme shall avoid it by as wide a margin as is practicable.

(i) A vessel engaged in fishing shall not impede the passage of any vessel following a traffic lane.

(j) A vessel of less than 20 metres in length or a sailing vessel shall not impede the safe passage of a power driven vessel following a traffic lane.

(k) A vessel Restricted in her Ability to Manoeuvre when engaged in an operation for the maintenance of safety of navigation in a traffic separating scheme is exempted from complying with this Rule to the extent necessary to carry out the operation.

(l) A vessel Restricted in her Ability to Manoeuvre when engaged in an operation for the laying, servicing or picking up a submarine cable, within a traffic separating scheme, is exempted from complying with

this Rule to the extent necessary to carry out the operation.

Section II – Conduct of Vessels in Sight of One Another

Rule 11: *Application*

Rules in this section apply to vessels in sight of one another.

Rule 12: *Sailing Vessels*

(a) When two sailing vessels are approaching one another, so as to involve risk of collision, one of them shall keep out of the way of the other as follows:

   (i) When each of them has the wind on a different side, the vessel which has the wind on the port side shall keep out of the way of the other;

   (ii) When both have the wind on the same side, the vessel which is to windward shall keep out of the way of the vessel which is to leeward;

   (iii) If the vessel with the wind on the port side sees a vessel to windward and cannot determine with certainty whether the other vessel has the wind on the port or the starboard side, she shall keep out of the way of the other.

(b) For the purposes of this Rule the windward side shall be deemed to be the side opposite to that on which the mainsail is carried or, in the case of a square rigged vessel, the side opposite to that on which the largest fore-and-aft sail is carried.

Rule 13: *Overtaking*

(a) Notwithstanding anything contained in the Rules of Part B, Sections I and II, any vessel overtaking any other shall keep out of the way of the vessel being overtaken.

12

(b) A vessel shall be deemed to be overtaking when coming up with a another vessel from a direction more than 22.5 degrees abaft her beam, that is, in such a position with reference to the vessel she is overtaking, that at night she would be able to see only the sternlight of that vessel but neither of her sidelights.

(c) When a vessel is in any doubt as to whether she is overtaking another, she shall assume that this is the case and act accordingly.

(d) Any subsequent alteration of the bearing between the two vessels shall not make the overtaking vessel a crossing vessel within the meaning of these Rules or relieve her of the duty of keeping clear of the overtaken vessel until she is finally past and clear.

Rule 14: *Head-on Situation*

(a) When two power-driven vessels are meeting on reciprocal or nearly reciprocal courses so as to involve risk of collision each shall alter her course to starboard so that each shall pass on the port side of the other.

(b) Such a situation shall be deemed to exist when a vessel sees the other ahead or nearly ahead and by night she could see the masthead lights in line or nearly in line and/or both sidelights and by day she observes the corresponding aspect of the other vessel.

(c) When a vessel is in any doubt as to whether such a situation exists she shall assume that it does exist and act accordingly.

Rule 15: *Crossing Situation*

When two power-driven vessels are crossing so as to involve risk of collision, the vessel which has the other on her own starboard side shall keep out of the way and shall, if the circumstances of the case admit, avoid crossing ahead of the other vessel.

Rule 16: *Action by Give-way Vessel*

Every vessel which is directed to keep out of the way of another vessel shall, so far as possible, take early and substantial action to keep well clear.

Rule 17: *Action by Stand-on Vessel*

(a)

   (i) Where one of two vessels is to keep out of the way of the other shall keep her course and speed.

   (ii) The latter vessel may however take action to avoid collision by her manoeuvre alone, as soon as it becomes apparent to her that the vessel required to keep out of the way is not taking appropriate action in accordance with these Rules.

(b) When, from any cause, the vessel required to keep her course and speed finds herself so close that collision cannot be avoided by the action of the give-way vessel alone, she shall take such action as will best aid to avoid collision.

(c) A power-driven vessel which takes action in a crossing situation in accordance with sub-paragraph (a)(ii) of this Rule to avoid collision with another power-driven vessel shall, if the circumstances of the case admit, not alter course to port for a vessel on her own port side.

(d) This Rule does not relieve the give-way vessel of her obligation to keep out of the way.

Rule 18: *Responsibilities between Vessels*

Except where rule 9, 10, and 13 otherwise require:

(a) A power driven vessel under way shall keep out of the way of:

   (i) A vessel not under command;

   (ii) A vessel restricted in her ability to manoeuvred;

(iii) A vessel engaged in fishing;

(iv) A sailing vessel;

(b) A sailing vessel under way shall keep out of the way of:

(i) A vessel not under command;

(ii) A vessel restricted in her ability to manoeuvre;

(iii) A vessel engaged in fishing;

(c) A vessel engaged in fishing when underway shall, so far as possible, keep out of the way of:

(i) A vessel not under command;

(ii) A vessel restricted in her ability to manoeuvre;

(d)

(i) Any vessel other than a vessel Not Under Command or a vessel Restricted in her Ability to Manoeuvre shall, if the circumstances of the case admit, avoid impeding the safe passage of a vessel Constrained by her Draft, exhibiting the signals in Rule 28.

(ii) A vessel Constrained by her Draft shall navigate with particular caution having full regard to her special condition.

(e) A seaplane on the water shall, in general, keep well clear of all vessels and avoid impeding their navigation. In circumstances, however, where risk of collision exists, she shall comply with the Rules of this Part.

(f)

(i) A WIG craft shall, when taking off, landing and in flight near the surface, keep well clear of all other vessels and avoid impeding their navigation.

(ii) A WIG craft operating on the water surface shall comply with the Rules of this Part as a power-driven vessel.

Section III – Conduct of Vessels in Restricted Visibility

Rule 19: *Conduct of Vessels in Restricted Visibility*

(a) This rule applies to vessels not in sight of one another when navigating in or near an area of restricted visibility.

(b) Every vessel shall proceed at a safe speed adapted to the prevailing circumstances and condition of restricted visibility. A power-driven vessel shall have her engines ready for immediate manoeuvre.

(c) Every vessel shall have due regard to the prevailing circumstances and conditions of restricted visibility when complying with the Rules of Section I of this Part.

(d) A vessel which detects by radar alone the presence of another vessel shall determine if a close-quarters situation is developing and/or risk of collision exists. If so, she shall take avoiding action in ample time, provided that when such action consists of an alteration in course, so far as possible the following shall be avoided:

(i) An alteration of course to port for a vessel forward of the beam, other than for a vessel being overtaken;

(ii) An alteration of course toward a vessel abeam or abaft the beam.

(e) Except where it has been determined that a risk of collision does not exist, every vessel which hears apparently forward of her beam the fog signal of another vessel, or which cannot avoid a close-quarters situation with another vessel forward of her beam, shall reduce her speed to be the minimum at which she can be kept on her course. She shall if necessary take all her way off and in any event navigate with extreme caution until danger of collision is over.

12

Part C – Lights and Shapes

Rule 20: *Application*

(a) Rules in this part shall be complied with in all weathers.

(b) The Rules concerning lights shall be complied with from sunset to sunrise, and during such times no other lights shall be exhibited, except such lights which cannot be mistaken for the lights specified in these Rules or do not impair their visibility or distinctive character, or interfere with the keeping of a proper look-out.

(c) The lights prescribed by these rules shall, if carried, also be exhibited from sunrise to sunset in restricted visibility and may be exhibited in all other circumstances when it is deemed necessary.

(d) The Rules concerning shapes shall be complied with by day.

(e) The lights and shapes specified in these Rules shall comply with the provisions of Annex I to these Regulations.

Rule 21: *Definitions*

(a) "Masthead light" means a white light placed over the fore and aft centreline of the vessel showing an unbroken light over an arc of horizon of 225 degrees and so fixed as to show the light from right ahead to 22.5 degrees abaft the beam on either side of the vessel.

(b) "Sidelights" means a green light on the starboard side and a red light on the port side each showing an unbroken light over an arc of horizon of 112.5 degrees and so fixed as to show the light from right ahead to 22.5 degrees abaft the beam on the respective side. In a vessel of less than 20 metres in length the sidelights may be combined in one lantern carried on the fore and aft centreline of the vessel.

(c) "Sternlight", means a white light placed as nearly as practicable at the stern showing an unbroken light over an arc of horizon of 135 degrees and so fixed as to show the light 67.5 degrees from right aft on each side of the vessel.

(d) "Towing light" means a yellow light having the same characteristics as the "sternlight" defined in paragraph (c) of this Rule.

(e) "All round light" means a light showing an unbroken light over an arc of horizon of 360 degrees.

(f) "Flashing light" means a light flashing at regular intervals at a frequency of 120 flashes or more per minute.

Rule 22: *Visibility of Lights*

The lights prescribed in these Rules shall have an intensity as specified in Section 8 of Annex I to these Regulations so as to be visible at the following minimum ranges:

(a) In vessels of 50 metres or more in length:
- a masthead light, 6 miles;
- a sidelight, 3 miles;
- a sternlight, 3 miles
- a towing light, 3 miles;
- a white red, green or yellow all-around light, 3 miles.

(b) In vessels of 12 metres or more in length but less than 50 metres in length;

  (i) a masthead light, 5 miles; except that where the length of the vessel is less than 20 metres, 3 miles;

  (ii) a sidelight, 2 miles;

  (iii) a sternlight, 2 miles,

  (iv) a towing light, 2 miles;

  (v) a white, red, green or yellow all-round light, 2 miles.

(c) In vessels of less than 12 metres in length:

- a masthead light, 2 miles;
- a sidelight, 1 mile;
- a sternlight, 2 miles;
- a towing light, 2 miles;
- a white red, green or yellow all-around light, 2 miles.

(d) In inconspicuous, partly submerged vessels or objects being towed;

- a white all-round light; 3 miles.

Rule 23: *Power-driven Vessels Underway*

(a) A power-driven vessel underway shall exhibit:

  (i) A masthead light forward;

  (ii) A second masthead light abaft of and higher than the forward one; except that a vessel of less than 50 metres in length shall not be obliged to exhibit such a light but may do so;

  (iii) Sidelights:

  (iv) A sternlight.

(b) An air-cushion vessel when operating in non-displacement mode shall, in addition to the lights prescribed in paragraph (a) of this Rule, exhibit an all-round flashing yellow light.

(c) A WIG craft only when taking off, landing and in flight near the surface shall, in addition to the lights prescribed in paragraph (i) of this Rule, exhibit a high intensity all-round flashing red light.

(d)

  (i) A power-driven vessel of less than 12 metres in length may in lieu of the lights prescribed in paragraph (a) of this Rule exhibit an all-round white light and sidelights

  (ii) A power-driven vessel of less than 7 metres in length whose maximum speed does not exceed 7 knots may in lieu of the lights prescribed in paragraph (a) of this Rule exhibit an all-round white light and shall, if practicable, also exhibit sidelights.

  (iii) The masthead light or all-round white light on a power-driven vessel of less than 12 meters in length may be displaced from the fore and aft centreline of the vessel if centreline fitting is not practicable, provided the sidelights are combined in one lantern which shall be carried on the fore and aft centreline of the vessel or located as nearly as practicable in the same fore and aft line as the masthead light or all-round white light.

Rule 24: *Towing and Pushing*

(a) A power driven vessel when towing shall exhibit:

  (i) Instead of the light prescribed in Rule 23(a)(i) or (a)(ii), two masthead lights in a vertical line. When the length of the tow measuring from the stern of the towing vessel to the after end of the tow exceeds 200 metres, three such lights in a vertical line;

  (ii) Sidelights;

  (iii) A sternlight

  (iv) A towing light in a vertical line above the sternlight;

  (v) When the length of the tow exceeds 200 metres, a diamond shape where it can best be seen.

(b) When a pushing vessel and a vessel being pushed ahead are rigidly connected in a composite unit they shall be regarded as a power-driven vessel and exhibit the lights prescribed in Rule 23.

12

(c) A power-driven vessel when pushing ahead or towing alongside, except in the case of a composite unit, shall exhibit:

    (i) Instead of the light prescribed in Rule 23(a)(i) or (a)(ii), two masthead lights in a vertical line.

    (ii) Sidelights;

    (iii) A sternlight.

(d) A power-driven vessel to which paragraph (a) or (c) of this Rule apply shall also comply with rule 23(a)(ii).

(e) A vessel or object being towed, other than those mentioned in paragraph (g) of this Rule, shall exhibit:

    (i) Sidelights;

    (ii) A sternlight;

    (iii) When the length of the tow exceeds 200 metres, a diamond shape where it can best be seen.

(f) Provided that any number of vessels being towed alongside or pushed in a group shall be lighted as one vessel,

    (i) A vessel being pushed ahead, not being part of a composite unit, shall exhibit at the forward end, sidelights;

    (ii) A vessel being towed alongside shall exhibit a sternlight and at the forward end, sidelights.

(g) An inconspicuous, partly submerged vessel or object, or combination of such vessels or objects being towed, shall exhibit:

    (i) If it is less than 25 metres in breadth, one all-round white light at or near the front end and one at or near the after end except that dracones need not exhibit a light at or near the forward end;

    (ii) If it is 25 metres or more in breadth, two or more additional all-round white lights at or near the extremities of its breadth;

    (iii) If it exceeds 100 metres in length, additional all-round white lights between the lights prescribed in subparagraphs (i) and (ii) so that the distance between the lights shall not exceed 100 metres;

    (iv) A diamond shape at or near the aftermost extremity of the last vessel or object being towed and if the length of the tow exceeds 200 metres an additional diamond shape where it can best be seen and located as far forward as is practicable.

(h) When from any sufficient cause it is impracticable for a vessel or object being towed to exhibit the lights or shapes prescribed in paragraph (e) or (g) of this Rule, all possible measures shall be taken to light the vessel or object being towed or at least indicate the presence of such vessel or object.

(i) Where from any sufficient cause it is impracticable for a vessel not normally engaged in towing operations to display the lights prescribed in paragraph (a) or (c) of this Rule, such vessel shall not be required to exhibit those lights when engaged in towing another vessel in distress or otherwise in need of assistance. All possible measures shall be taken to indicate the nature of the relationship between the towing vessel and the vessel being towed as authorised by Rule 36, in particular to illuminate the towline.

Rule 25: *Sailing Vessels Underway and Vessels Under Oars*

(a) A sailing vessel underway shall exhibit:

    (i) Sidelights;

    (ii) A sternlight.

(b) In a sailing vessel of less than 20 metres in length the lights prescribed in paragraph (a) of this Rule may be combined in one lantern carried at or near the top of the mast where it can best be seen.

(c) A sailing vessel underway may, in addition to the lights prescribed in paragraph (a) of this Rule, exhibit at or near the top of the mast, where they can best be seen, two all-round lights in a vertical line, the upper being red and the lower green, but these lights shall not be exhibited in conjunction with the combined lantern permitted by paragraph (b) of this Rule.

(d)

   (i) A sailing vessel of less than 7 metres in length shall, if practicable, exhibit the lights prescribed in paragraph (a) or (b) of this Rule, but if she does not, she shall have ready at hand an electric torch or lighted lantern showing a white light which shall be exhibited in sufficient time to prevent collision.

   (ii) A vessel under oars may exhibit the lights prescribed in this Rule for sailing vessels, but, if she does not, she shall have ready at hand an electric torch or lighted lantern showing a white light which shall be exhibited in sufficient time to prevent collision.

(e) A vessel proceeding under sail when also being propelled by machinery shall exhibit forward where it can best be seen a conical shape, apex downwards.

Rule 26: Fishing Vessels

(a) A vessel engaged in fishing, whether underway or at anchor, shall exhibit only the lights and shapes prescribed by this rule.

(b) A vessel when engaged in trawling, by which is meant the dragging through the water of a dredge net or other apparatus used as a fishing appliance, shall exhibit;

   (i) Two all-round lights in a vertical line, the upper being green and the lower white, or a shape consisting of two cones with their apexes together in a vertical line one above the other;

   (ii) A masthead light abaft of and higher than the all-round green light; a vessel of less than 50 metres in length shall not be obliged to exhibit such a light but may do so;

   (iii) When making way through the water, in addition to the lights prescribed in this paragraph, sidelights and a sternlight.

(c) A vessel engaged in fishing, other than trawling, shall exhibit:

   (i) Two all-round lights in a vertical line, the upper being red and the lower white, or a shape consisting of two cones with their apexes together in a vertical line one above the other.

   (ii) When there is outlying gear extending more than 150 metres horizontally from the vessel, an all-round white light or a cone apex upwards in the direction of the gear.

   (iii) When making way through the water, in addition to the lights prescribed in this paragraph, sidelights and a sternlight.

(d) The additional signals described in Annex II to these Regulations apply to a vessel engaged in fishing in close proximity to other vessels engaged in fishing.

(e) A vessel when not engaged in fishing shall not exhibit the lights or shapes prescribed in this Rule, but only those prescribed for a vessel of her length.

Rule 27: *Vessels Not Under Command or Restricted in Their Ability to Manoeuvre*

(a) A vessel Not Under Command shall exhibit:

(i) Two all-round red lights in a vertical line where they can best be seen;

(ii) Two balls or similar shapes in a vertical line where they can best be seen;

(iii) When making way through the water, in addition to the lights prescribed in this paragraph, sidelights and a sternlight.

(b) A vessel Restricted in her Ability to Manoeuvre, except a vessel engaged in mine clearance operations, shall exhibit:

(i) Three all-round lights in a vertical line where they can best be seen. The highest and lowest of these lights shall be red and the middle light shall be white;

(ii) Three shapes in a vertical line where they can best be seen. The highest and lowest of these shapes shall be balls and the middle one a diamond.

(iii) When making way through the water, masthead light or lights, sidelights and a sternlight in addition to the lights prescribed in sub-paragraph (i);

(iv) When at anchor, in addition to the lights or shapes prescribed in sub-paragraphs (i) and (ii), the light, lights, or shape prescribed in Rule 30.

(c) A power-driven vessel engaged in a towing operation such as severely restricts the towing vessel and her tow in their ability to deviate from their course shall, in addition to the lights or shapes prescribed in Rule 24(a), exhibit the lights or shapes prescribed in subparagraph (b)(i) and (ii) of this Rule.

(d) A vessel engaged in dredging or underwater operations, when Restricted in her Ability to Manoeuvre, shall exhibit the lights and shapes prescribed in sub-paragraphs (b)(i), (ii) and (iii) of this Rule and shall in addition when an obstruction exists, exhibit:

(i) Two all-round red lights or two balls in a vertical line to indicate the side on which the obstruction exists;

(ii) Two all-round green lights or two diamonds in a vertical line to indicate the side on which another vessel may pass;

(iii) When at anchor, the lights or shapes prescribed in this paragraph instead of the lights or shapes prescribed in Rule 30.

(e) Whenever the size of a vessel engaged in diving operations makes it impracticable to exhibit all lights and shapes prescribed in paragraph (d) of this Rule, the following shall be exhibited:

(i) Three all-round lights in a vertical line where they can best be seen. The highest and lowest of these lights shall be red and the middle light shall be white;

(ii) A rigid replica of the International Code flag "A" not less than 1 metre in height. Measures shall be taken to ensure its all-round visibility.

(f) A vessel engaged in mine clearance operations shall in addition to the lights prescribed for a power-driven vessel in

Rule 23 or for a vessel at anchor in Rule 30 as appropriate, exhibit three all-round green lights or three balls. One of these lights or shapes shall be exhibited near the foremast head and one at each end of the fore yard. These lights or shapes indicate that it is dangerous for another vessel to approach within 1000 metres of the mine clearance vessel.

(g) Vessels of less than 12 metres in length, except those engaged in diving operations, shall not be required to exhibit the lights prescribed in this Rule.

(h) The signals prescribed in this Rule are not signals of vessels in distress and requiring assistance. Such signals are contained in Annex IV to these Regulations.

Rule 28: *Vessels Constrained by their Draft*

A vessel Constrained by her Draft may, in addition to the lights prescribed for power-driven vessels in Rule 23, exhibit where they can best be seen three all-round red lights in a vertical line, or a cylinder.

Rule 29: *Pilot Vessels*

(a) A vessel engaged on pilotage duty shall exhibit:

   (i) At or near the masthead, two all-round lights in a vertical line, the upper being white and the lower red;

   (ii) When underway, in addition, sidelights and a sternlight;

   (iii) When at anchor, in addition to the lights prescribed in sub-paragraph (i), the light, lights or shape prescribed in Rule 30 for vessels at anchor.

(b) A pilot vessel when not engaged on pilotage duty shall exhibit the lights or shapes prescribed for a similar vessel of her length.

Rule 30: *Anchored Vessels and Vessels Aground*

(a) A vessel at anchor shall exhibit where it can best be seen:

   (i) In the fore part, an all-round white light or one ball;

   (ii) At or near the stern and at a lower level than the light prescribed in sub-paragraph (i), an all-round white light.

(b) A vessel of less than 50 metres in length may exhibit an all-round white light where it can best be seen instead of the lights prescribed in paragraph (a) of this Rule.

(c) A vessel at anchor may, and a vessel of 100 metres and more in length shall, also use the available working or equivalent lights to illuminate her decks.

(d) A vessel aground shall exhibit the lights prescribed in paragraph (a) or (b) of this Rule and in addition, where they can best be seen;

   (i) Two all-round red lights in a vertical line;

   (ii) Three balls in a vertical line.

(e) A vessel of less than 7 metres in length, when at anchor not in or near a narrow channel, fairway or where other vessels normally navigate, shall not be required to exhibit the shape prescribed in paragraphs (a) and (b) of this Rule.

(f) A vessel of less than 12 metres in length, when aground, shall not be required to exhibit the lights or shapes prescribed in sub-paragraphs (d)(i) and (ii) of this Rule.

Rule 31: *Seaplanes*

Where it is impracticable for a seaplane or a WIG craft to exhibit lights or shapes of the

12

characteristics or in the positions prescribed in the Rules of this Part she shall exhibit lights and shapes as closely similar in characteristics and position as is possible.

Part D – Sound and Light Signals

Rule 32: *Definitions*

(a) The word "whistle" means any sound signalling appliance capable of producing the prescribed blasts and which complies with the specifications in Annex III to these Regulations.

(b) The term "short blast" means a blast of about one second's duration.

(c) The term "prolonged blast" means a blast from four to six seconds' duration.

Rule 33: *Equipment for Sound Signals*

(a) A vessel of 12 metres or more in length shall be provided with a whistle, a vessel of 20 metres or more in length shall be provided with a bell in addition to a whistle, and a vessel of 100 metres or more in length shall, in addition, be provided with a gong, the tone and sound of which cannot be confused with that of the bell. The whistle, bell and gong shall comply with the specifications in Annex III to these Regulations. The bell or gong or both may be replaced by other equipment having the same respective sound characteristics, provided that manual sounding of the prescribed signals shall always be possible.

(b) A vessel of less than 12 metres in length shall not be obliged to carry the sound signalling appliances prescribed in paragraph (a) of this Rule but if she does not, she shall be provided with some other means of making an efficient signal.

Rule 34: *Manoeuvring and Warning Signals*

(a) When vessels are in sight of one another, a power-driven vessel under way, when manoeuvring as authorized or required by these Rules, shall indicate that manoeuvre by the following signals on her whistle:

- one short blast to mean "I am altering my course to starboard";
- two short blasts to mean "I am altering my course to port";
- three short blasts to mean "I am operating astern propulsion".

(b) Any vessel may supplement the whistle signals prescribed in paragraph (a) of this Rule by light signals, repeated as appropriate, whilst the manoeuvre is being carried out:

(i) These signals shall have the following significance:

- one flash to mean "I am altering my course to starboard";
- two flashes to mean "I am altering my course to port";
- three flashes to mean "I am operating astern propulsion".

(ii) The duration of each flash shall be about one second, the interval between flashes shall be about one second, and the interval between successive signals shall not be less than ten seconds.

(iii) The light used for this signal shall, if fitted, be an all-round white light, visible at a minimum range of 5 miles, and shall comply with the provisions of Annex I to these Regulations.

(c) When in sight of one another in a narrow channel or fairway:

    (i) A vessel intending to overtake another shall in compliance with Rule 9 (e)(i) indicate her intention by the following signals on her whistle.

        (i) two prolonged blasts followed by one short blast to mean "I intend to overtake you on your starboard side";

        (ii) two prolonged blasts followed by two short blasts to mean "I intend to overtake you on your port side".

    (ii) The vessel about to be overtaken when acting in accordance with 9(e)(i) shall indicate her agreement by the following signal on her whistle:

        ■ one prolonged, one short, one prolonged and one short blast, in that order.

(d) When vessels in sight of one another are approaching each other and from any cause either vessel fails to understand the intentions or actions of the other, or is in doubt whether sufficient action is being taken by the other to avoid collision, the vessel in doubt shall immediately indicate such doubt by giving at least five short and rapid blasts on the whistle. Such signal may be supplemented by at least five short and rapid flashes.

(e) A vessel nearing a bend or an area of a channel or fairway where other vessels may be obscured by an intervening obstruction shall sound one prolonged blast. Such signal shall be answered with a prolonged blast by any approaching vessel that may be within hearing around the bend or behind the intervening obstruction.

(f) If whistles are fitted on a vessel at a distance apart of more than 100 metres, one whistle only shall be used for giving manoeuvring and warning signals.

Rule 35: *Sound Signals in Restricted Visibility*

In or near an area of restricted visibility, whether by day or night the signals prescribed in this Rule shall be used as follows:

(a) A power-driven vessel making way through the water shall sound at intervals of not more than 2 minutes one prolonged blast.

(b) A power-driven vessel underway but stopped and making no way through the water shall sound at intervals of no more than 2 minutes two prolonged blasts in succession with an interval of about 2 seconds between them.

(c) A vessel Not Under Command, a vessel Restricted in her Ability to Manoeuvre, a vessel Constrained by her Draft, a sailing vessel, a vessel engaged in fishing and a vessel engaged in towing or pushing another vessel shall, instead of the signals prescribed in paragraph (a) or (b) of this Rule, sound at intervals of not more than 2 minutes three blasts in succession, namely one prolonged followed by two short blasts.

(d) A vessel engaged in fishing, when at anchor, and a vessel Restricted in her Ability to Manoeuvre when carrying out her work at anchor, shall instead of the signals prescribed in paragraph (g) of this Rule sound the signal prescribed in paragraph (c) of this Rule.

(e) A vessel towed or if more than one vessel is being towed the last vessel of the tow, if manned, shall at intervals of not more than 2 minutes sound four blasts in succession, namely one prolonged followed by three short blasts. When practicable, this signal shall be made immediately after the signal made by the towing vessel.

(f) When a pushing vessel and a vessel being pushed ahead are rigidly connected in a

12

12

composite unit they shall be regarded as a power-driven vessel and shall give the signals prescribed in paragraphs (a) or (b) of this Rule.

(g) A vessel at anchor shall at intervals of not more than one minute ring the bell rapidly for 5 seconds. In a vessel 100 metres or more in length the bell shall be sounded in the forepart of the vessel and immediately after the ringing of the bell the gong shall be sounded rapidly for about 5 seconds in the after part of the vessel. A vessel at anchor may in addition sound three blasts in succession, namely one short, one long and one short blast, to give warning of her position and of the possibility of collision to an approaching vessel.

(h) A vessel aground shall give the bell signal and if required the gong signal prescribed in paragraph (g) of this Rule and shall, in addition, give three separate and distinct strokes on the bell immediately before and after the rapid ringing of the bell. A vessel aground may in addition sound an appropriate whistle signal.

(i) A vessel of 12 metres or more, but less than 20 metres in length shall not be obliged to give the bell signals prescribed in paragraphs (g) and (h) of this Rule. However, if she does not, she shall make some other efficient sound signal at intervals of not more than 2 minutes.

(j) A vessel of less than 12 metres in length shall not be obliged to give the above-mentioned signals but, if she does not, shall make some other efficient sound signal at intervals of not more than 2 minutes.

(k) A pilotage vessel when engaged on pilotage duty may in addition to the signals prescribed in paragraph (a), (b) or (g) of this Rule sound an identity signal consisting of four short blasts.

Rule 36: *Signals to Attract Attention*

If necessary to attract the attention of another vessel, any vessel may make light or sound signals that cannot be mistaken for any signal authorized elsewhere in these Rules, or may direct the beam of her searchlight in the direction of the danger, in such a way as not to embarrass any vessel. Any light to attract the attention of another vessel shall be such that it cannot be mistaken for any aid to navigation. For the purpose of this Rule the use of high intensity intermittent or revolving lights, such as strobe lights, shall be avoided.

Rule 37: *Distress Signals*

When a vessel is in distress and requires assistance she shall use or exhibit the signals described in Annex IV to these Regulations.

Part E – Exemptions

Rule 38: *Exemptions*

Any vessel (or class of vessel) provided that she complies with the requirements of the International Regulations for the Preventing of Collisions at Sea, 1960, the keel of which is laid or is at a corresponding stage of construction before the entry into force of these Regulations may be exempted from compliance therewith as follows:

(a) The installation of lights with ranges prescribed in Rule 22, until 4 years after the date of entry into force of these regulations.

(b) The installation of lights with colour specifications as prescribed in Section 7 of Annex I to these Regulations, until four years after the date of entry into force of these Regulations.

(c) The repositioning of lights as a result of conversion from Imperial to metric units and rounding off measurement figures, permanent exemption.

(d)

    (i) The repositioning of masthead lights on vessels of less than 150 metres in length, resulting from the prescriptions of Section 3 (a) of Annex I to these regulations, permanent exemption.

    (ii) The repositioning of masthead lights on vessels of 150 metres or more in length, resulting from the prescriptions of Section 3 (a) of Annex I to these regulations, until 9 years after the date of entry into force of these Regulations.

(e) The repositioning of masthead lights resulting from the prescriptions of Section 2(b) of Annex I to these Regulations, until nine years after the date of entry into force of these Regulations.

(f) The repositioning of sidelights resulting from the prescriptions of Section 2(g) and 3(b) of Annex I to these Regulations, until nine years after the date of entry into force of these Regulations.

(g) The requirements for sound signal appliances prescribed in Annex III to these Regulations, until nine years after the date of entry into force of these Regulations.

(h) The repositioning of all-round lights resulting from the prescription of Section 9(b) of Annex I to these Regulations, permanent exemption.

ANNEX I

Positioning and technical details of lights and shapes

1. *Definition*

The term "height above the hull" means height above the uppermost continuous deck. This height shall be measured from the position vertically beneath the location of the light.

2. *Vertical positioning and spacing of lights*

(a) On a power-driven vessel of 20 metres or more in length the masthead lights shall be placed as follows:

    (i) The forward masthead light, or if only one masthead is carried, then that light, at a height above the hull of not less than 6 metres, and, if the breadth of the vessel exceeds 6 metres, then at a height above the hull not less than such breadth, so however that the light need not to be placed at a greater height above the hull than 12 metres.

    (ii) When two masthead lights are carried the after one shall be at least 4.5 metres vertically higher than the forward one.

(b) The vertical separation of masthead lights of power-driven vessels shall be such that in all normal conditions of trim the after light will be seen over and separate from the forward light at a distance o 1,000 metres from the stern when viewed from sea level.

(c) The masthead light of a power-driven vessel of 12 metres but less than 20 metres in length shall be placed at a height above the gunwale of not less than 2.5 metres.

(d) A power-driven vessel of less than 12 metres in length may carry the uppermost light at a height of less than 2.5 metres above the gunwale. When however a masthead light is carried in addition to sidelights and a sternlight or the all-round light of Rule 23(c)(i) is carried in addition to sidelights, then such masthead light or all-round light shall be carried at least 1 metre higher than the sidelights.

(e) One of the two or three masthead lights prescribed for a power-driven vessel when engaged in towing or pushing another

12

vessel shall be placed in the same position as either the forward masthead light or the after masthead light; provided that, if carried on the aftermast, the lowest after masthead light shall be at least 4.5 metres vertically higher than the forward masthead light.

(f)

(i) The masthead light or lights prescribed in Rule 23 (a) shall be so placed as to be above and clear of all other lights and obstructions except as described in sub-paragraph (ii).

(ii) When it is impracticable to carry the all-round lights prescribed by Rule 27(b)(i) or Rule 28 below the masthead lights, they may be carried above the after masthead light(s) or vertically in between the forward masthead light(s) and after masthead light(s), provided that in the later case the requirement of Section 3(c) of this Annex shall be complied with.

(g) The sidelights of a power-driven vessel shall be placed at a height above the hull not greater than three-quarters of that of the forward masthead light. They shall not be so low as to be interfered with by deck lights.

(h) The sidelights if in a combined lantern and carried on a power-driven vessel of less than 20 metres in length, shall be placed not less than 1 metre below the masthead light.

(i) When the Rules prescribe two or three lights to be carried in a vertical line, shall be spaced as follows:

(i) On a vessel of 20 metres or more such lights shall be spaced not less than 2 metres apart, and the lowest of these lights shall, except where a towing light is required, be placed at a height of not less than 4 metres above the hull.

(ii) On a vessel of less than 20 metres in length such lights shall be spaced not less than 1 metre apart and the lowest of these lights shall, except where a towing light is required, be placed at a height of not than 2 metres above the gunwale;

(iii) When three lights are carried they shall be equally spaced.

(j) The lower of the two all-round lights prescribed for a vessel when engaged in fishing shall be at a height above the sidelights not less than twice the distance between the two vertical lights.

(k) The forward anchor light prescribed in Rule 30 (a)(i), when two are carried, shall not be less than 4.5 metres above the after one. On a vessel of 50 metres or more in length this forward anchor light shall be placed at a height of not less than 6 metres above the hull.

3. Horizontal positioning and spacing of lights

(a) When two masthead lights are prescribed for a power-driven vessel, the horizontal distance between them shall not be less than one-half of the length of the vessel but need not be more than 100 metres. The forward light shall be placed not more than one-quarter of the length of the vessel from the stern.

(b) On a power-driven vessel of 20 metres or more in length the sidelights shall not be placed in front of the forward masthead lights. They shall be placed at or near the side of the vessel.

(c) When the lights prescribed in Rule 27(b)(i) or Rule 28 are placed vertically between the forward masthead light(s) and the after masthead light(s) these all-round lights shall be placed at a horizontal distance of not less than 2 metres from the fore and aft centerline of the vessel in the athwartship direction.

(d) When only one masthead light is prescribed for a power-driven vessel, this light shall be exhibited forward of amidships; except that a vessel less than 20 metres in length need not exhibit this light forward of amidships but shall exhibit it as far forward as practicable.

4. Details of location of direction-indicating lights for fishing vessels, dredgers and vessel engaged in underwater operations

(a) The light indicating the direction of the outlying gear from a vessel engaged in fishing as prescribed in Rule 26(c)(ii) shall be placed at a horizontal distance of not less than 2 metres and not more than 6 metres away from the two all-round red and white lights. This light shall be placed not higher than the all-round white light prescribed in Rule 26(c)(i) and not lower than the sidelights.

(b) The lights and shapes on a vessel engaged in dredging or under water operations to indicate the obstructed side and/or the side on which it is safe to pass, as prescribed in Rule 27(d)(i) and (ii), shall be placed at the minimum practical horizontal distance, but in no case less than 2 metres, from the lights or shapes prescribed in Rule 27(b)(i) and (ii). In no case shall the upper of these lights or shapes be at a greater height than the lower of the three lights or shapes prescribed in Rule 27(b)(i) and (ii).

5. Screens for sidelights

The sidelights of vessel of 20 metres or more in length shall be fitted with inboard screens painted matt black, and meeting requirements of section 9 of this Annex. On vessel of less than 20 metres in length the sidelights, if necessary to meet the requirements of Section 9 of this Annex, shall be fitted with inboard matt black screens. With a combined lantern, using a single vertical filament and a very narrow division between the green and red sections, external screens need not be fitted.

6. Shapes

(a) Shapes shall be black and of the following sizes:

  (i) A ball shall have a diameter of not less than 0.6 metre;

  (ii) A cone shall have a base diameter of not less than 0.6 metre and a height equal to its diameter.

  (iii) A cylinder shall have a diameter of at least 0.6 metre and a height of twice its diameter;

  (iv) A diamond shape shall consist of two cones as defined in (ii) above having a common base.

(b) The vertical distance between shapes shall be at least 1.5 metres.

(c) In a vessel of less than 20 metres in length shapes of lesser dimensions but commensurate with the size of the vessel may be use and the distance apart may be correspondingly reduced.

7. Colour specification of lights

The chromaticity of all navigation lights shall confirm to the following standards, which lie within the boundaries of the area of the diagram specified for each colour are given by indicating Commission on Illumination (CIE).

The boundaries of the area for each colour are given by indicating the corner co-ordinates, which are as follows:

(i)   *White*

x 0.525 0.525 0.452 0.310 0.310 0.443
y 0.382 0.440 0.440 0.348 0.283 0.382

(ii) *Green*

x   0.028   0.009   0.300   0.203
y   0.385   0.723   0.511   0.356

(iii) *Red*

x   0.680   0.660   0.735   0.721
y   0.320   0.320   0.265   0.259

(iv) *Yellow*

x   0.612   0.618   0.575   0.575
y   0.382   0.382   0.425   0.406

8. Intensity of lights

(a) The minimum luminous intensity f lights shall be calculated by using the formula:

$I = 3.43 \times 10^6 \times T \times D^2 \times K{-}D$

Where I = luminous intensity in candles under service conditions,

T is threshold factor 2×10^{-7} lux,

D is range of visibility (luminous range) of the light in nautical miles,

K is atmospheric transmissivity,

For prescribed lights the value of K shall be 0.8, corresponding to a meteorological visibility of approximately 13 nautical miles.

(b) A selection of figures derived from the formula is given in the following table:

Range of visibility (luminous range) of light in nautical miles	Luminous intensity of light in candelas for K = 0.8
D	I
1	0.9
2	4.3
3	12
4	27
5	52
6	94

Note. The maximum luminous intensity of navigation lights should be limited to avoid undue glare. This shall not be achieved by a variable control of the luminous intensity.

9. Horizontal sectors

(a)

(i)   In the forward direction, sidelights as fitted on the vessel shall show the minimum required intensities. The intensities shall decrease to reach practical cut-off between 1 degree and 3 degree outside the prescribed sectors.

(ii) For sternlights and masthead lights and at 22.5 degrees abaft the beam for side lights, the minimum required intensities shall be maintained over the arc of the horizon up to 5 degrees within the limits of the sectors prescribed in Rule 21. From 5 degrees within the prescribed sectors the intensity may decrease by 50 per cent up to the prescribed limits; it shall decrease steadily to reach practical cut-off at not more than 5 degrees outside the prescribed sectors.

(b)

(i) All-round lights shall be so located as not to be obscured by masts, topmasts or structures within angular sectors of more than 6 degrees, except anchor lights prescribed in Rule 30, which need not be placed at an impracticable height above the hull.

(ii) If it is impracticable to comply with paragraph (b)(i) of this section by exhibiting only one all-round light, two all-round lights shall be used suitably positioned or screened so that they appear, as far as practicable, as one light at a distance of one mile.

10. Vertical sectors

(a) The vertical sectors of electric lights as fitted, with the exemption of lights on sailing vessels underway shall ensure that:

(i) At least the required minimum intensity is maintained at all angles from 5 degrees above to 5 degrees below the horizontal;

(ii) At least 60 per cent of the required minimum intensity is maintained from 7.5 degrees above to 7.5 degrees below the horizontal;

(b) In the case of sailing vessels underway the vertical sectors of electric lights as fitted shall ensure that;

(i) At least the required minimum intensity is maintained at all angles

from 5 degrees above to 5 degrees below the horizontal;

(ii) At least 50 per cent of the required minimum intensity is maintained from 25 degrees above to 5 degrees below the horizontal.

(c) In the case of lights other than electric these specifications shall be met as closely as possible.

11. Intensity of non-electric lights

Non electric lights shall so far as practicable comply with the minimum intensities, as specified in the Table given in Section 8 of this Annex.

12. Manoeuvring Light

Notwithstanding the provisions of paragraph 2(f) of this Annex the manoeuvring light described in rule 34(b) shall be placed in the same fore and aft vertical plane as the masthead light or lights and, where practicable, at a minimum height of 2 metres vertically above the forward masthead light, provided that it shall be carried not less than 2 metres vertically above or below the after masthead light. On a vessel where only one masthead light is carried the manoeuvring light, if fitted, shall be carried where it can best be seen, not less than 2 metres vertically apart from the masthead light.

13. High sped craft

(a) The masthead light of high speed craft may be placed at a height related to the breadth of the craft lower than that prescribed in paragraph 2(a)(i) of this Annex, provided that the base angle of the isosceles triangles formed by the sidelights and masthead light, when seen in end elevation, is not less than 27°.

12

(b) On high speed craft of 50 metres or more in length, the vertical separation between foremast and mainmast light of 4.5 metres required by paragraph 2(a)(ii) of this Annex may be modified provided that such distance shall not be less than the value determined by the following formula:

$$y = \frac{(a + 17\Psi)C}{1000} + 2$$

Where: y is the height of the mainmast light above the foremast light in metres

a is the height of the foremast light above the water surface in service condition in metres

Ψ is the trim in service condition in degrees

C is the horizontal separation of masthead lights in metres.

14. Approval

The constitution of lights and shapes and the installation of lights on board the vessel shall be to the satisfaction of the appropriate authority of the State whose flag the vessel is entitled to fly.

ANNEX II

Additional signals for fishing vessels fishing in close proximity

1. General

The lights mentioned herein shall, if exhibited in pursuance of Rule 26(d), be placed where they can best be seen. They shall be at least 0.9 metres apart but at a lower level than lights prescribed in Rule 26(b)(i) and (c)(i). The lights shall be visible all round the horizon at a distance of at least 1 mile but at a lesser distance than the lights prescribed by these Rules for fishing vessels.

2. Signals for trawlers

(a) Vessels of 20 metres or more in length when engaged in trawling, whether using demersal or pelagic gear, shall exhibit:

   (i)   When shooting their nets: two white lights in a vertical line

   (ii) When hauling their nets: one white light over one red light in a vertical line

   (iii) When the net has come fast upon an obstruction: two red lights in a vertical line

(b) Each vessel of 20 metres or more in length engaged in pair trawling shall exhibit:

   (i)   By night, a searchlight directed forward and in the direction of the other vessel of the pair.

   (ii) When shooting or hauling their nets or when their nets have come fast upon an obstruction, the lights prescribed in 2(a) above.

(c) A vessel of less than 20 m in length engaged in trawling, whether using demersal or pelagic gear or engaged in pair trawling, may exhibit the lights prescribed in paragraphs (a) or (b) of this section, as appropriate.

3. Signals for purse seiners

Vessels engaged in fishing with purse seine gear may exhibit two yellow lights in a vertical line. These lights shall flash alternately every second and with equal light and occultation duration. These lights may be exhibited only when the vessel is hampered by its fishing gear.

ANNEX III

Technical details of sound signal appliances

1. Whistles

(a) Frequencies and range of audibility

The fundamental frequency of the signal shall lie within the range of 70–700Hz. The range of audibility of the signal from a whistle shall be determined by those frequencies, which may include the fundamental and/or one or more higher frequencies, which lie within the range 180–700Hz ($\pm$1%) for a vessel of 20 metres or more in length, or 180–2100Hz ($\pm$1%) for a vessel of less than 20 metres in length and which provide the sound pressure levels specified in paragraph 1(c) below.

(b) Limits of fundamental frequencies

To ensure a wide variety of whistle characteristics, the fundamental frequency of a whistle shall be between the following limits:

   (i)   70–200Hz, for a vessel 200 metres or more in length;

   (ii) 130–350Hz, for a vessel 75 metres but less than 200 metres in length;

   (iii) 250–700Hz, for a vessel less than 75 metres in length.

(c) Sound signal intensity and range of audibility

A whistle fitted in a vessel shall provide, in the direction of maximum intensity of the whistle and at a distance of 1 metre from it, a sound pressure level in at least one 1/3rd –octave band within the range of frequencies 180–700Hz ($\pm$1%) for a vessel of 20 metres or more in length, or 180–2100Hz ($\pm$1%) for a vessel of less than 20 metres in length, of not less than the appropriate figure given in the table below.

Length of vessel in metres	1/3rd-octave band level at 1 metre in dB referred to 2×10^{-5} N/m²	Audibility range in nautical miles
200 or more	143	2
75, but less than 200	138	1.5
20, but less than 75	130	1
Less than 20	120*1	0.5
	115*2	
	100*3	

*1   When the measured frequencies lie within the range 180–450 Hz

*2   When the measured frequencies lie within the range 450–800 Hz

*3   When the measured frequencies lie within the range 800–2100 Hz

(d) Directional properties

The sound pressure level of a directional whistle shall be not more than 4 dB below the prescribed sound pressure level on the axis at any direction in the horizontal plane within $\pm$45 degrees of the axis. The sound pressure level at any other direction in the horizontal plane shall be not less than 10 dB below the prescribed sound pressure level on the axis, so that the range in any direction will be at least half the range on the forward axis. The sound pressure level shall be measured in that 1/3rd –octave band which determines the audibility range.

(e) Positioning of whistles

When a directional whistle is to be used as the only whistle on a vessel, it shall be installed with its maximum intensity directed straight ahead.

12

A whistle shall be placed as high as practicable on a vessel, in order to reduce interception of the emitted sound by obstructions and also to minimise hearing damage risk to personnel. The sound pressure level of the vessel's own signal at listening posts shall not exceed 110 dB (A) and so far as practicable should not exceed 100 dB (A).

(f) Fitting of more than one whistle

If whistles are fitted at a distance apart of more than 100 metres, it shall be so arranged that they are not sounded simultaneously.

(g) Combined whistle systems

If due to the pressure of obstructions the sound field of a single whistle or of one of the whistle referred to in paragraph 1(f) above is likely to have to have a zone of greatly reduced signal level, it is recommended that a combined whistle system be fitted so as to overcome this reduction. For the purpose of the Rules a combined whistle system is to be regarded as a single whistle. The whistles of a combined system shall be located at a distance apart of not more than 100 metres and arranged to be sounded simultaneously. The frequency of any one whistle shall differ from those of the others by at least 10Hz.

(h) Bell or gong

(a) Intensity of signal

A bell or gong, or other device having similar sound characteristics shall produce a sound pressure level of not less than 110dB at a distance of 1 metre from it.

(b) Construction

Bells and gongs shall be made of corrosion-resistant material and designed to give a clear tone. The diameter of the mouth of the bell shall be not less than 300mm for vessels of 20 meters or more in length. Where practicable, a power-driven bell-striker is recommended to ensure constant force but manual operation shall be possible. The mass of the striker shall not be less than 3 per cent of the mass of the bell.

3. Approval

The construction of sound signal appliances, their performance and their installation on board the vessel shall be to the satisfaction of the appropriate authority of the State whose flag the vessel is entitled to fly.

ANNEX IV

Distress signals

1   The following signals, used or exhibited either together or separately, indicate distress and need of assistance:

   (a)   A gun or other explosive signal fired at intervals of about a minute;

   (b)   A continuous sounding with any fog-signalling apparatus;

   (c)   Rockets or shells, throwing red stars fired one at a time at short intervals;

   (d)   A signal made by radiotelegraphy or by any other signalling method consisting of the group . . . - - - . . . (SOS) in the Morse Code;

   (e)   A signal made by radiotelegraphy consisting of the spoken word "Mayday";

   (f)   The International Code Signal of distress indicated by NC;

   (g)   A signal consisting of a square flag having above or below it a ball or anything resembling a ball;

   (h)   Flames on the vessel (as from a burning tar barrel, oil barrel, etc,);

(i) A rocket parachute flare or a hand flare showing a red light;

(j) A smoke signal giving off orange-coloured smoke;

(k) Slowly and repeatedly raising and lowering arms outstretched to each side;

(l) The radiotelegraph alarm signal;

(m) The radiotelephone alarm signal;

(n) Signals transmitted by emergency position indicating radio beacons;

(o) Approved signals transmitted by radio-communications systems including survival craft radar transponders;

2 The use or exhibition of any of the foregoing signals except for the purpose of indicating distress and need of assistance and the use of other signals which may be confused with any of the above signals is prohibited.

3 Attention is drawn to the relevant sections of the International Code of Signals, the Merchant Ship Search and Rescue Manual and the following signals:

(a) A piece of orange-coloured canvas with either a black square and circle or other appropriate symbol (for identification from the air);

(b) A dye marker.

12

12

List of Amendments

The 1981 amendments
Adoption: 19 November 1981
Entry into force: 1 June 1983

A number of rules are affected but perhaps the most important change concerns Rule 10, which has been amended to enable vessels carrying out various safety operations, such as dredging or surveying, to carry out these functions in traffic separation schemes.

The 1987 amendments
Adoption: 19 November 1987
Entry into force: 19 November 1989

The amendments affect several rules, including rule 1(e)? vessels of special construction: the amendment classifies the application of the Convention to such ships; Rule 3(h), which defines a vessel constrained by her draught; Rule 10(c)? crossing traffic lanes.

The 1989 amendments
Adoption: 19 October 1989
Entry into force: 19 April 1991

The amendment concerns Rule 10 and is designed to stop unnecessary use of the inshore traffic zone.

The 1993 amendments
Adoption: 4 November 1993
Entry into force: 4 November 1995

The amendments are mostly concerned with the positioning of lights.

The 2001 amendments
Adoption: 29 November 2001
Entry into force: 29 November 2003

The amendments include new rules relating to Wing-in Ground (WIG) craft. The following are amended:

General Definitions (Rule 3) – to provide the definition of wing-in-ground (WIG) craft;

- Action to avoid collision (Rule 8 (a)) – to make it clear that any action to avoid collision should be taken in accordance with the relevant rules in the COLREGs and to link Rule 8 with the other steering and sailing rules;

- Responsibilities between vessels (Rule 18) – to include a requirement that a WIG craft, when taking off, landing and in flight near the surface, shall keep clear of all other vessels and avoid impeding their navigation and also that a WIG craft operating on the water surface shall comply with the Rules as for a power-driven vessel;

- Power-driven vessels underway (Rule 23) – to include a requirement that WIG craft shall, in addition to the lights prescribed in paragraph 23 (a) of the Rule, exhibit a high-intensity all-round flashing red light when taking off, landing and in-flight near the surface;

- Seaplanes (Rule 31) – to include a provision for WIG craft;

- Equipment for sound signals and sound signals in restricted visibility (Rules 33 and 35) – to cater for small vessels;

- Positioning and technical details of lights and shapes (Annex I) – amendments with respect to high-speed craft (relating to the vertical separation of masthead lights); and

- Technical details of sound signal appliances (Annex III) – amendments with respect to whistles and bell or gong to cater for small vessels.